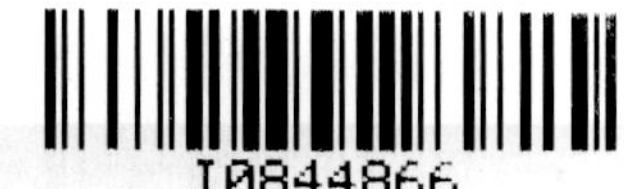

WELCOME TO THiS CREATiVE ADVENTURE

MANDALAS

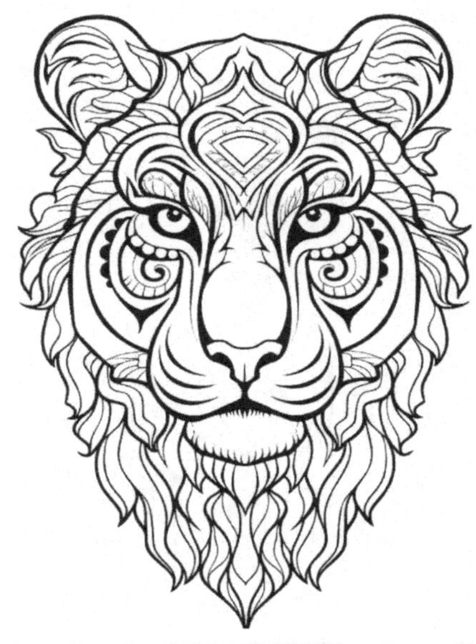

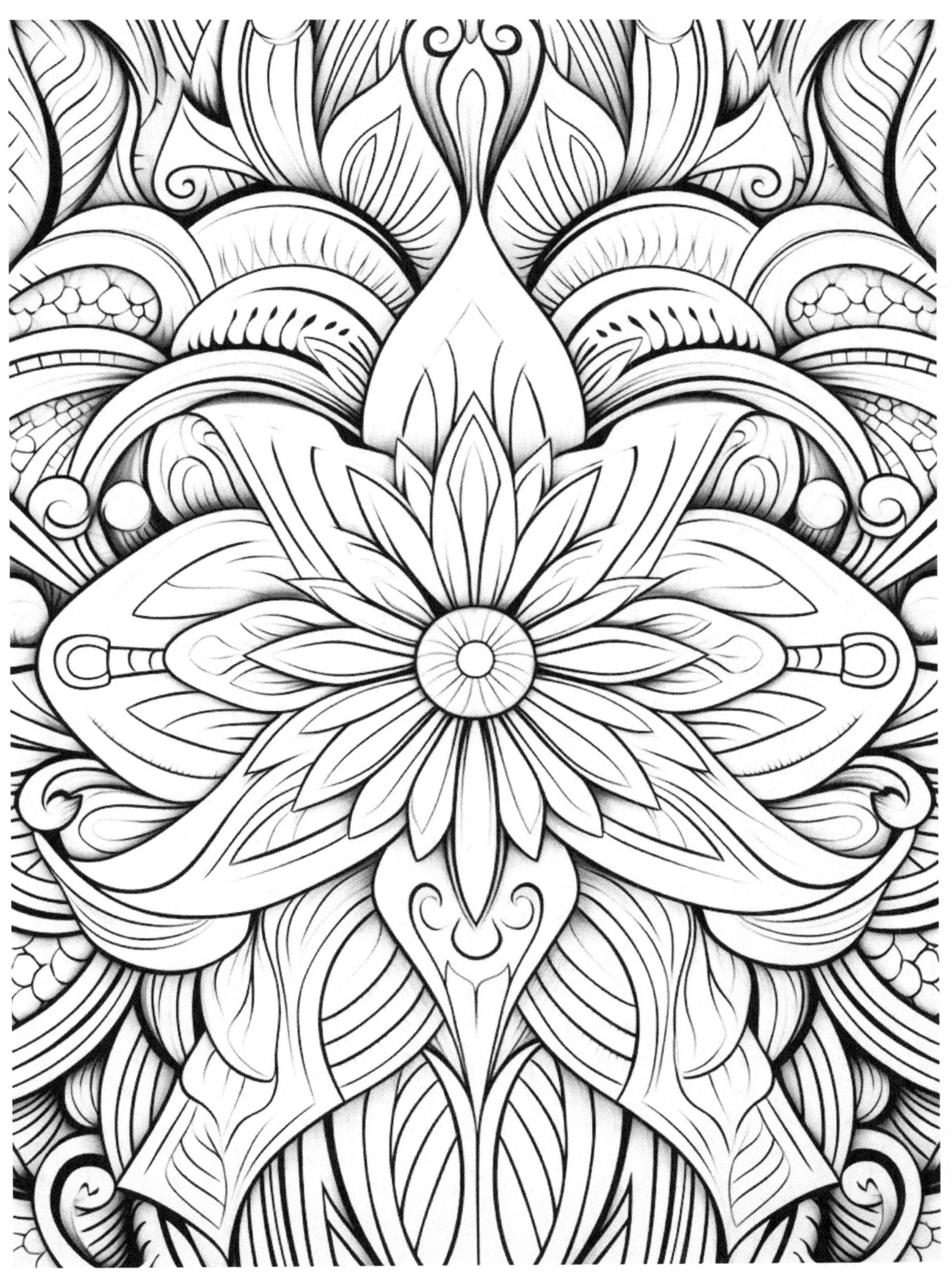

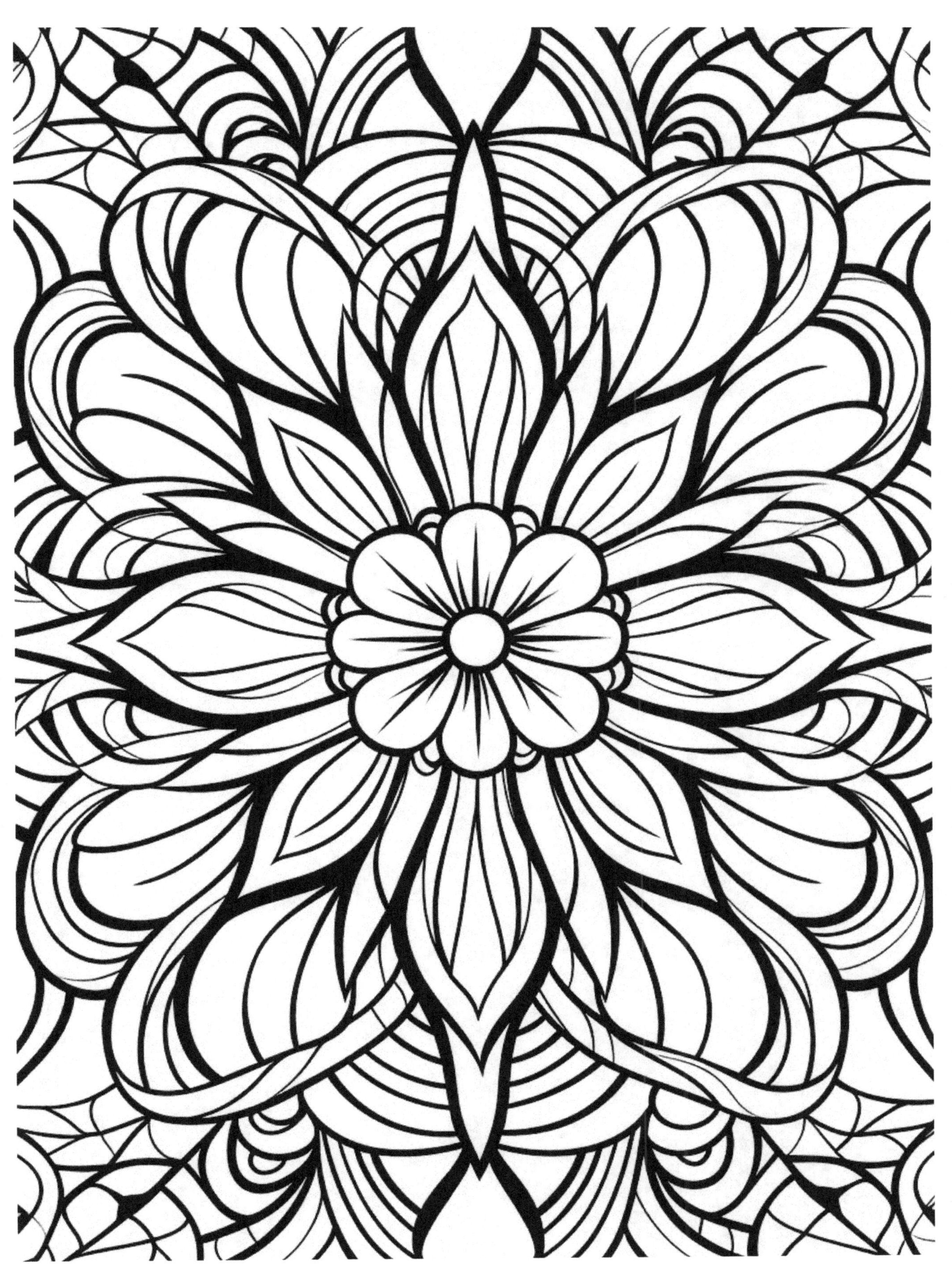

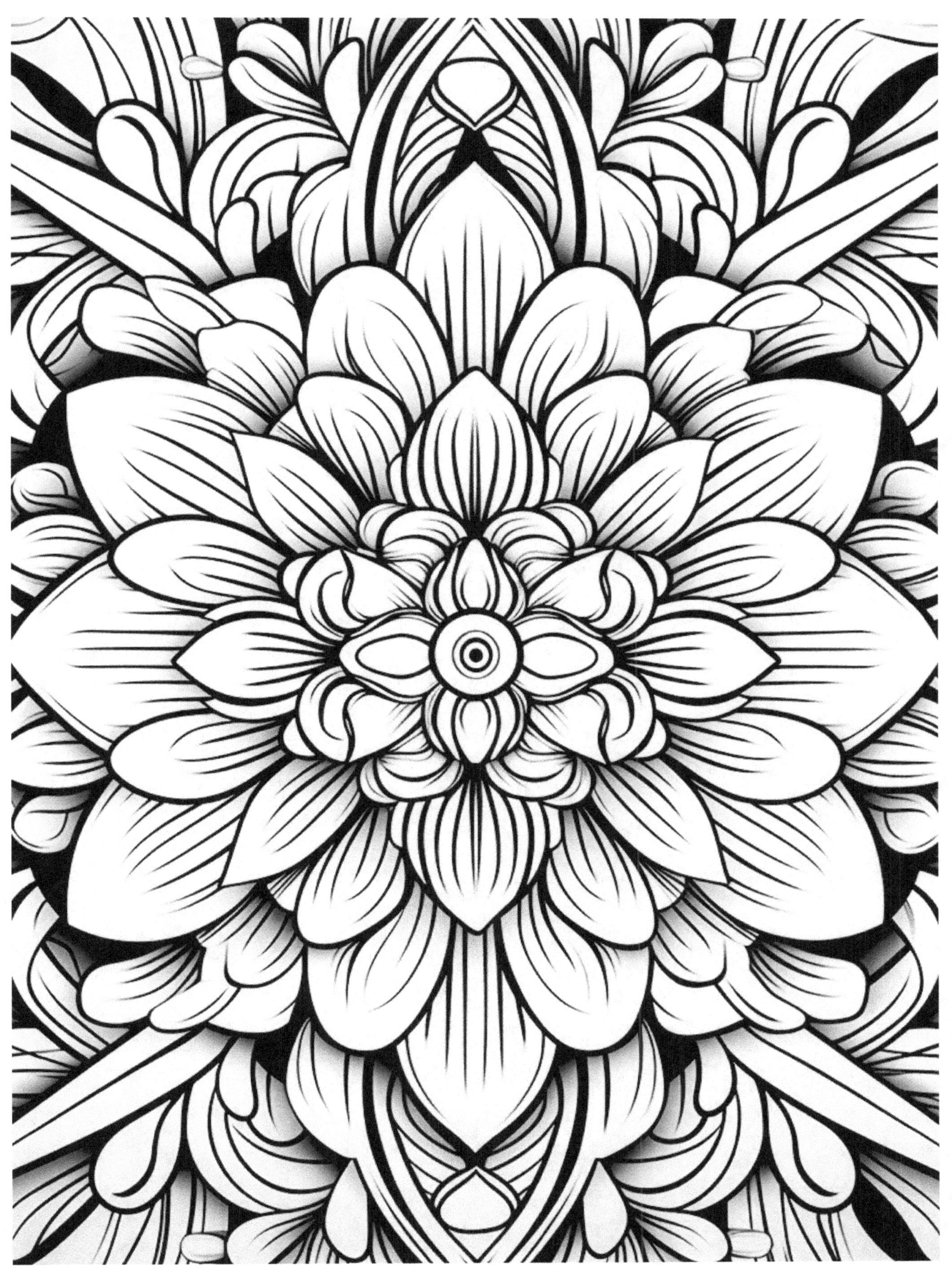

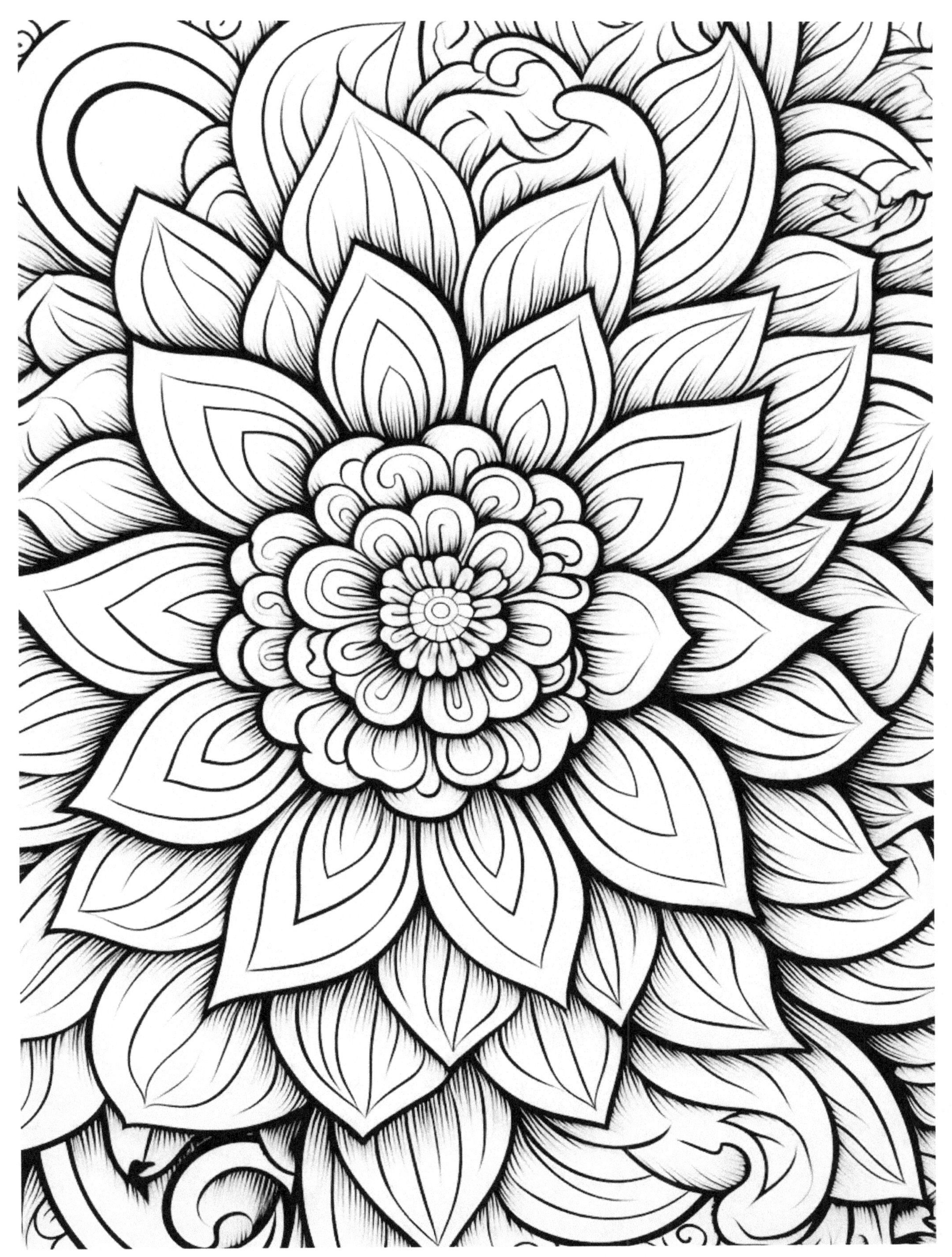

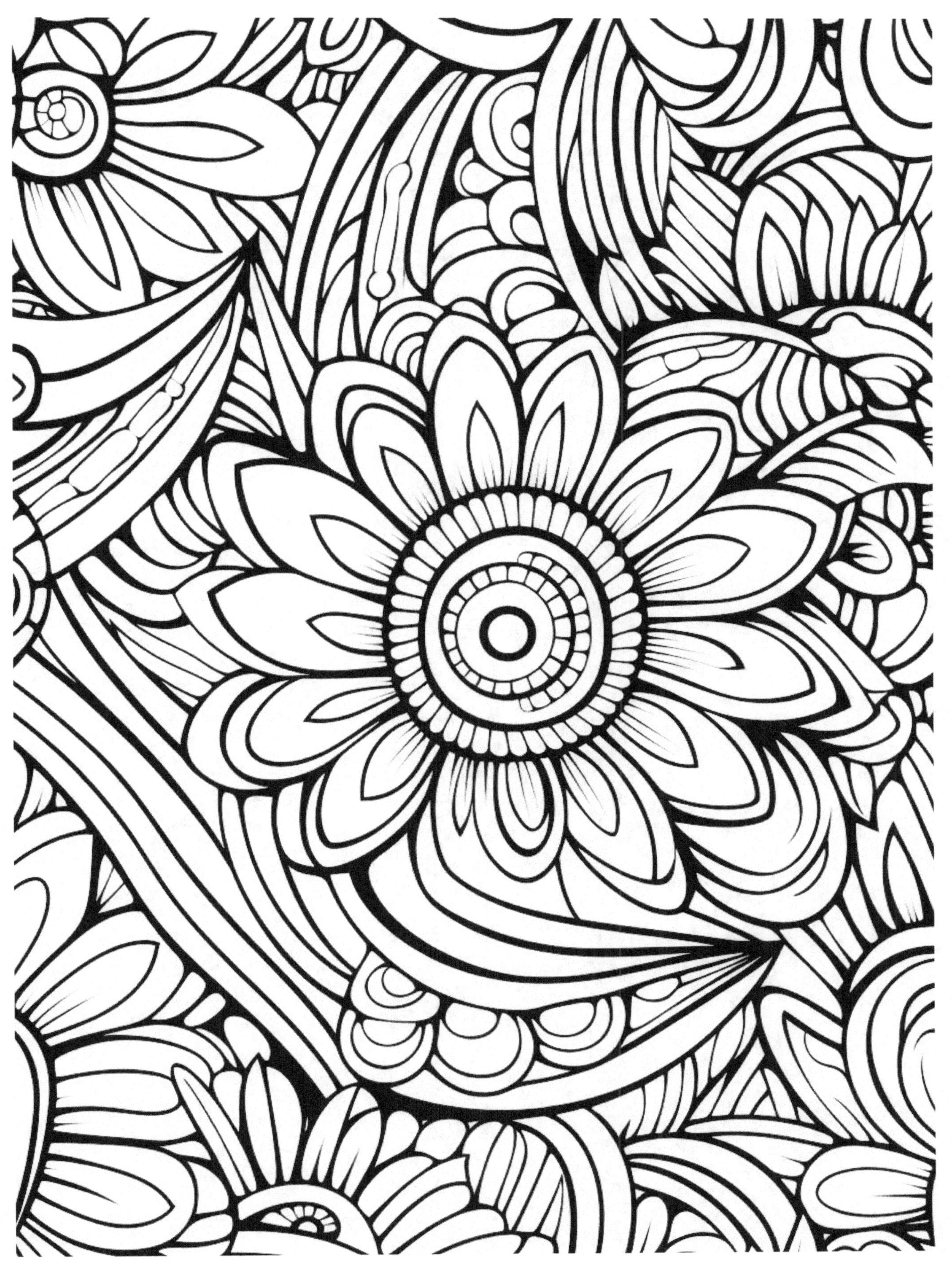

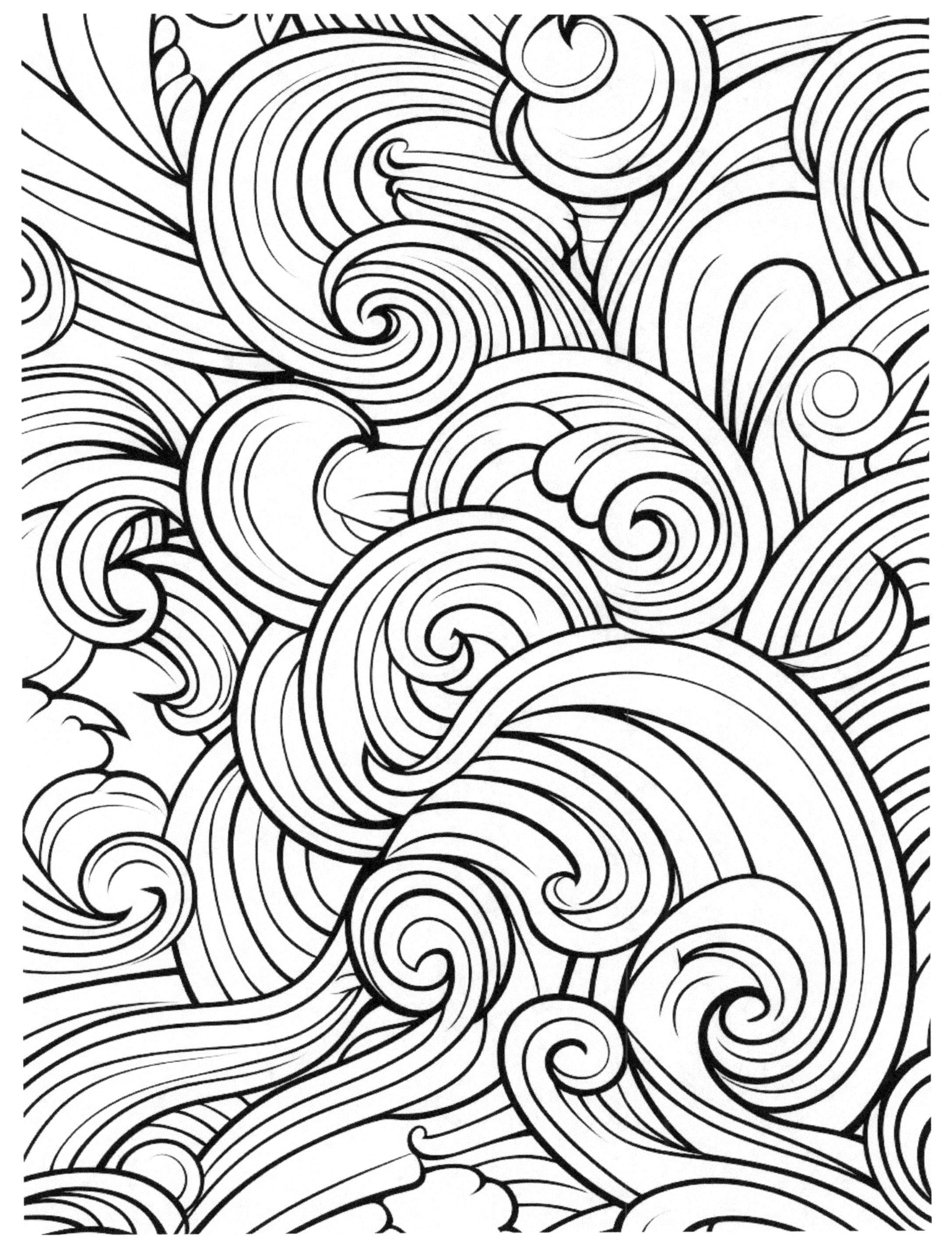

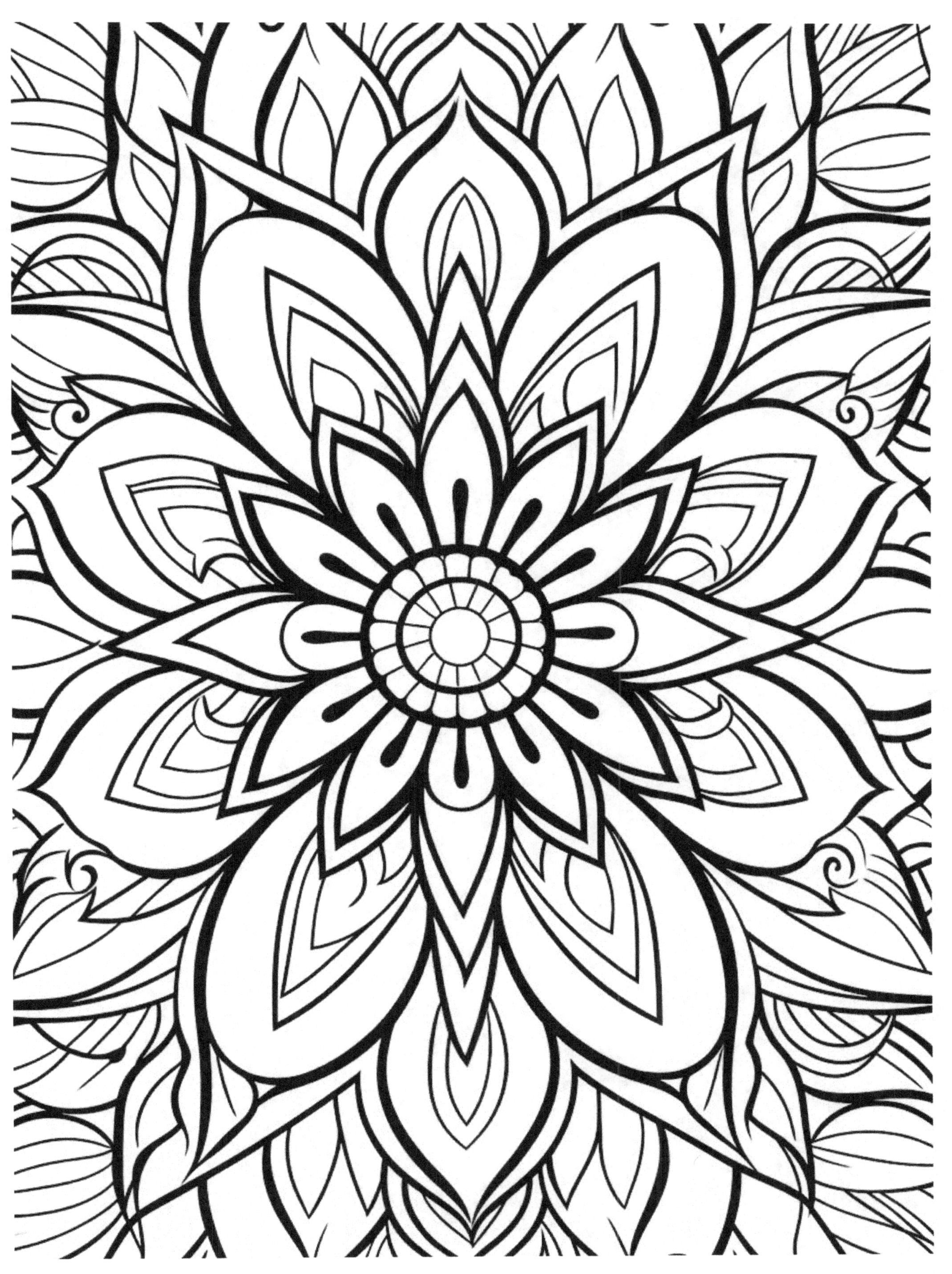

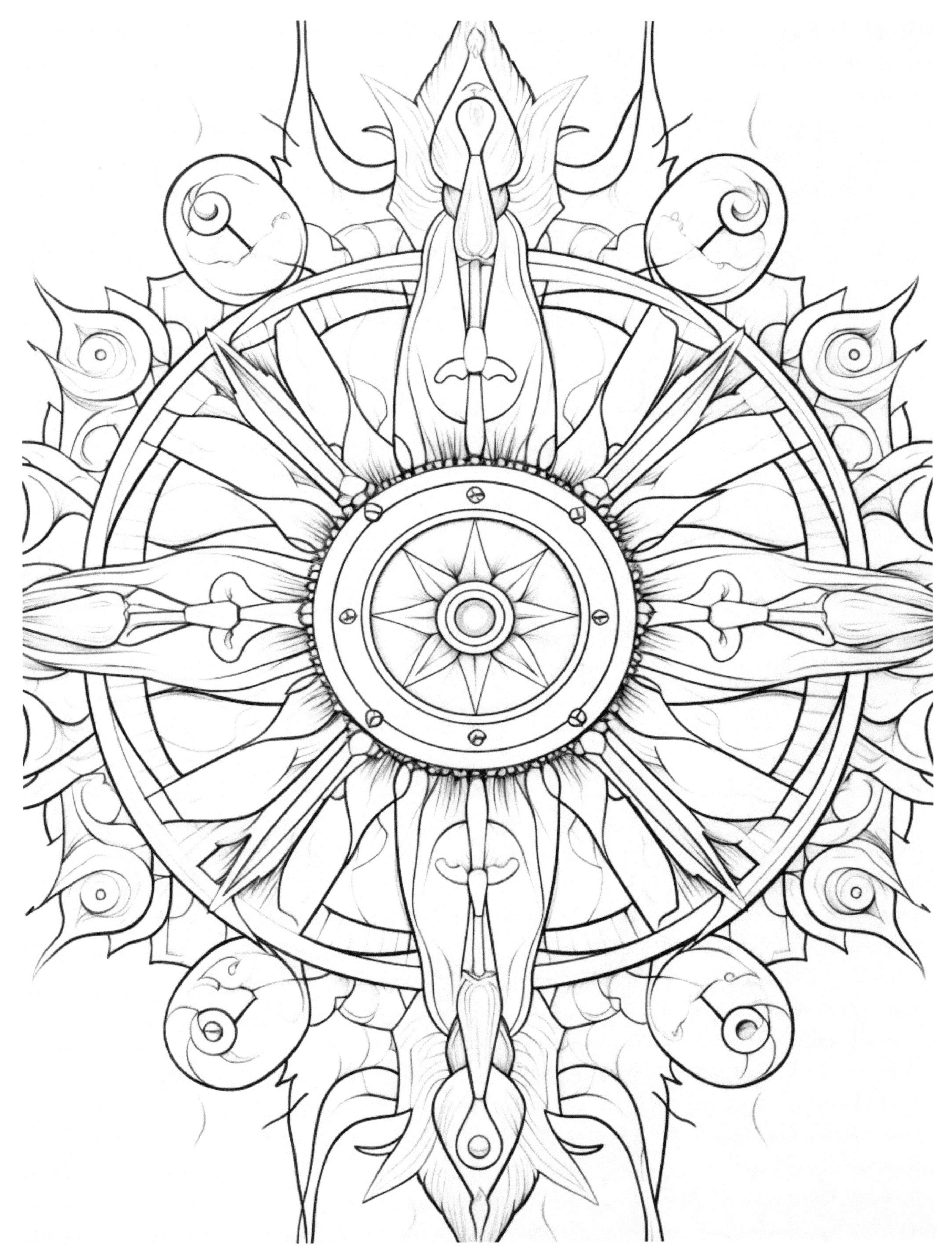

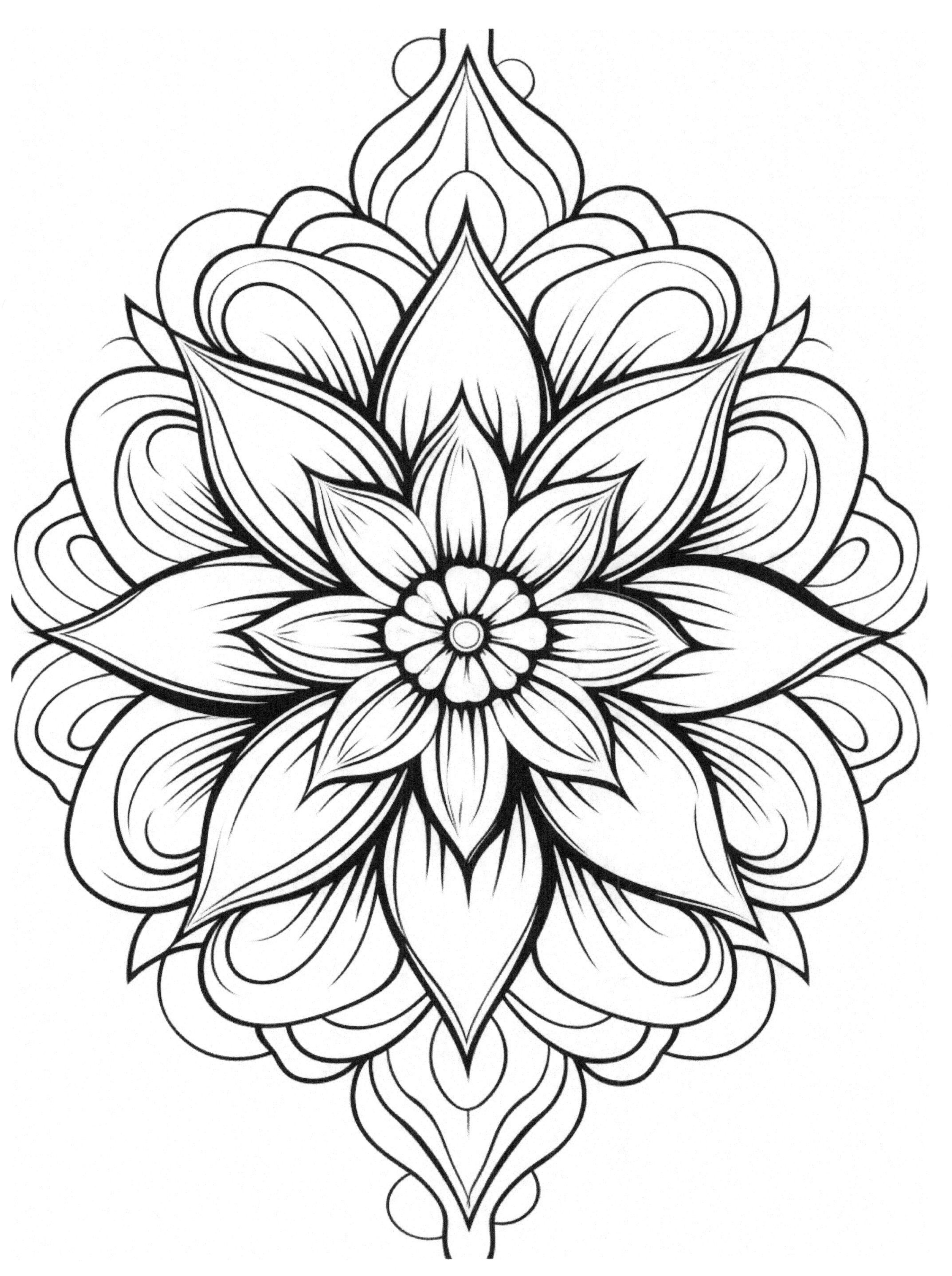

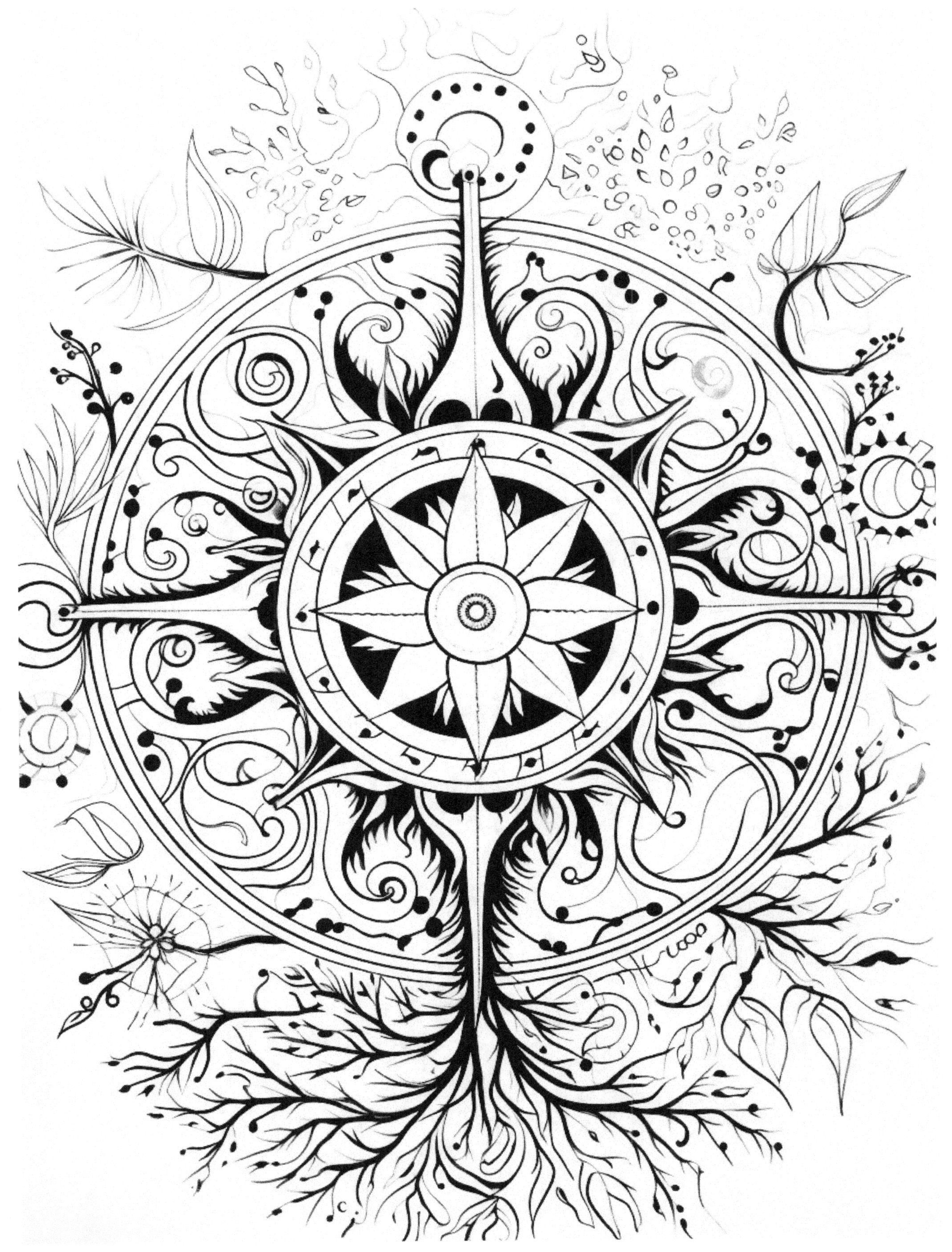

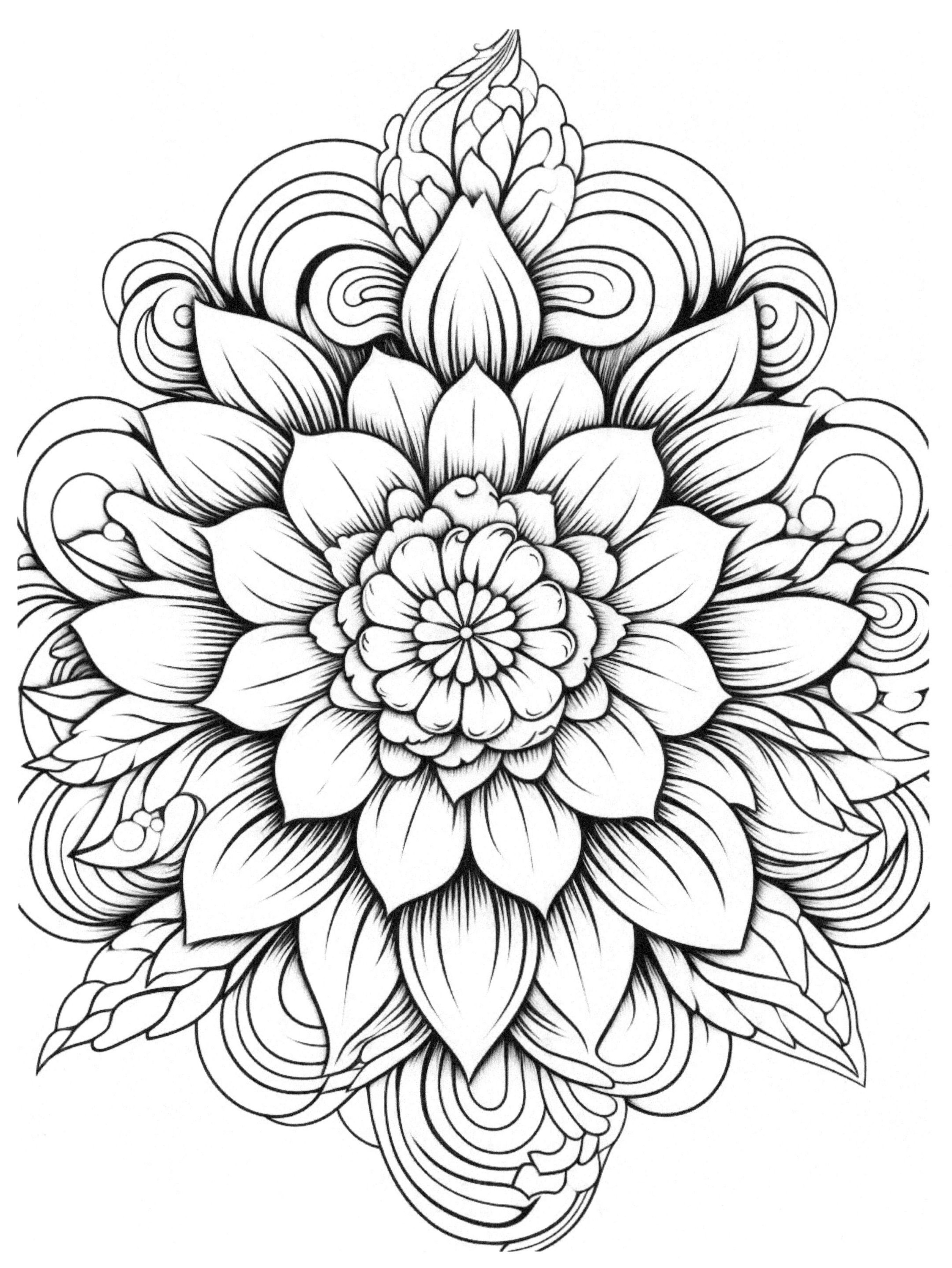

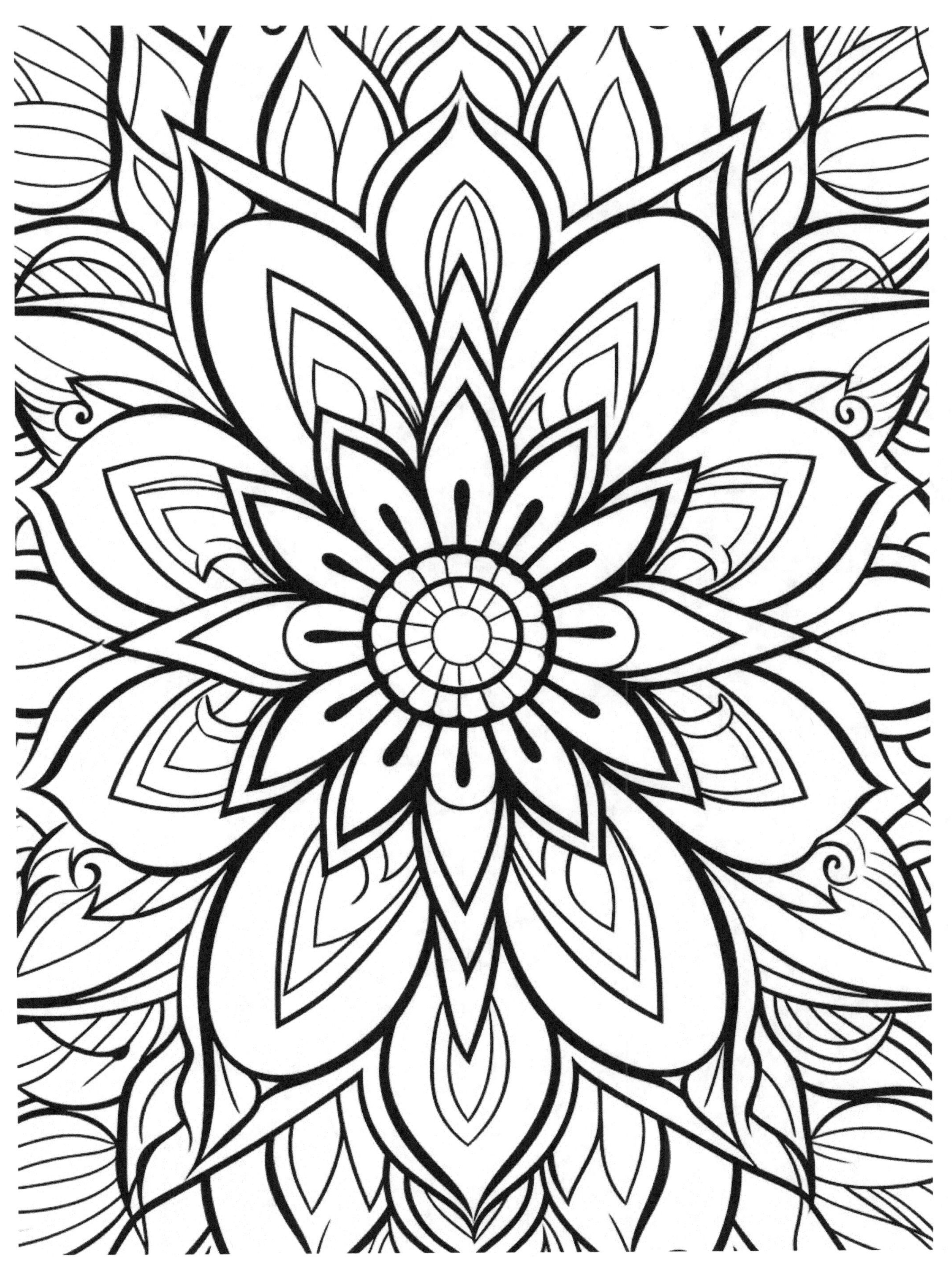

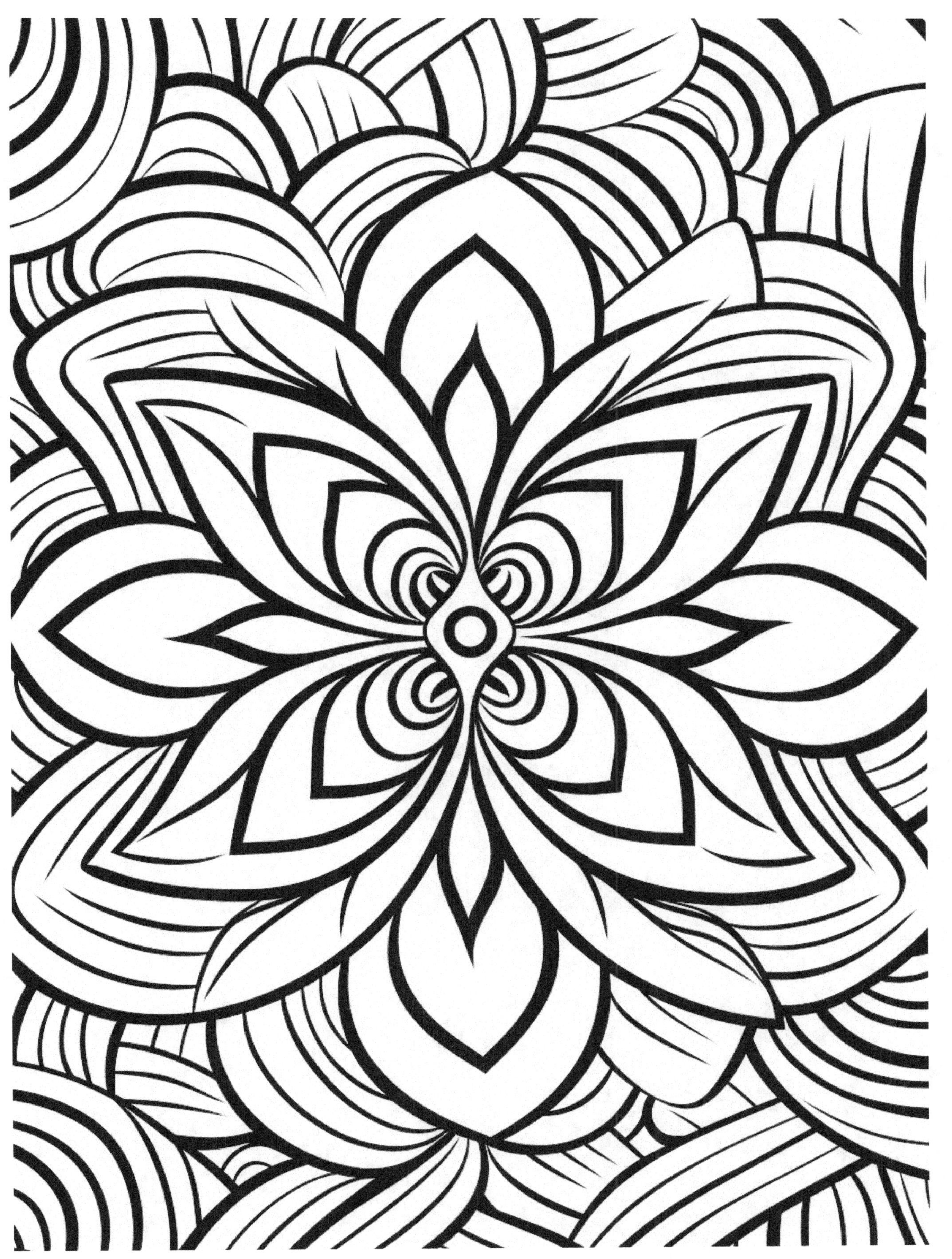

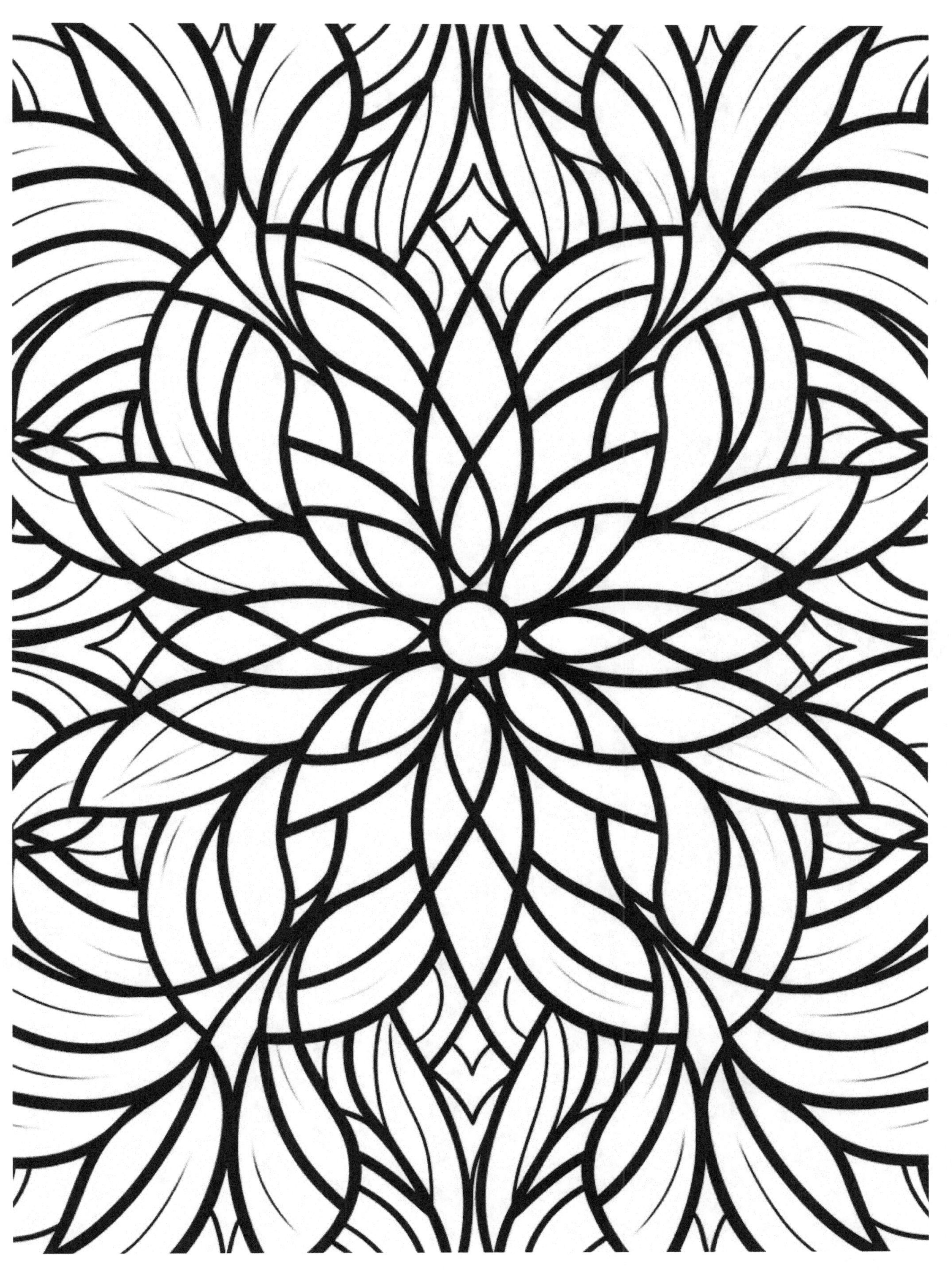

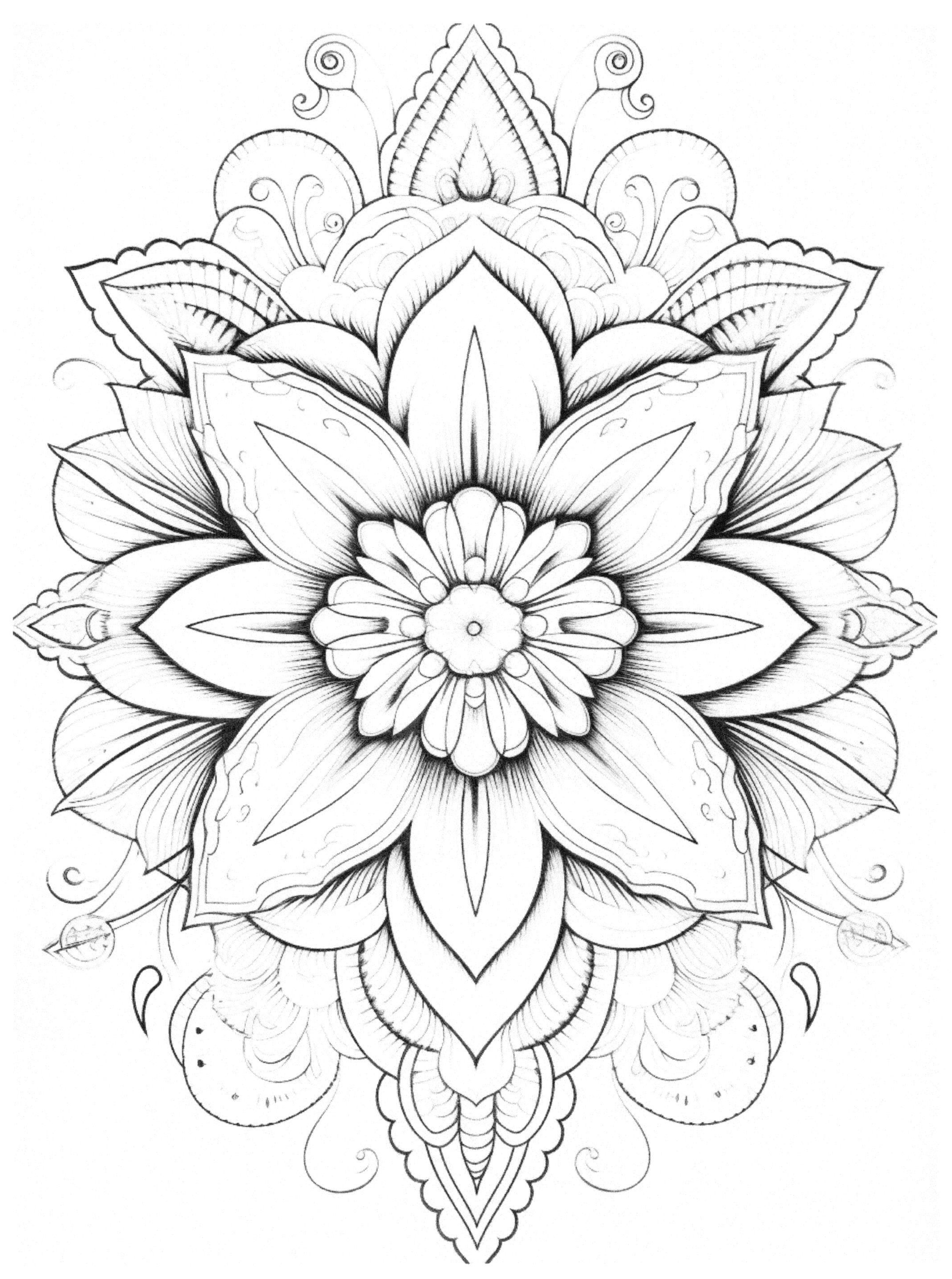

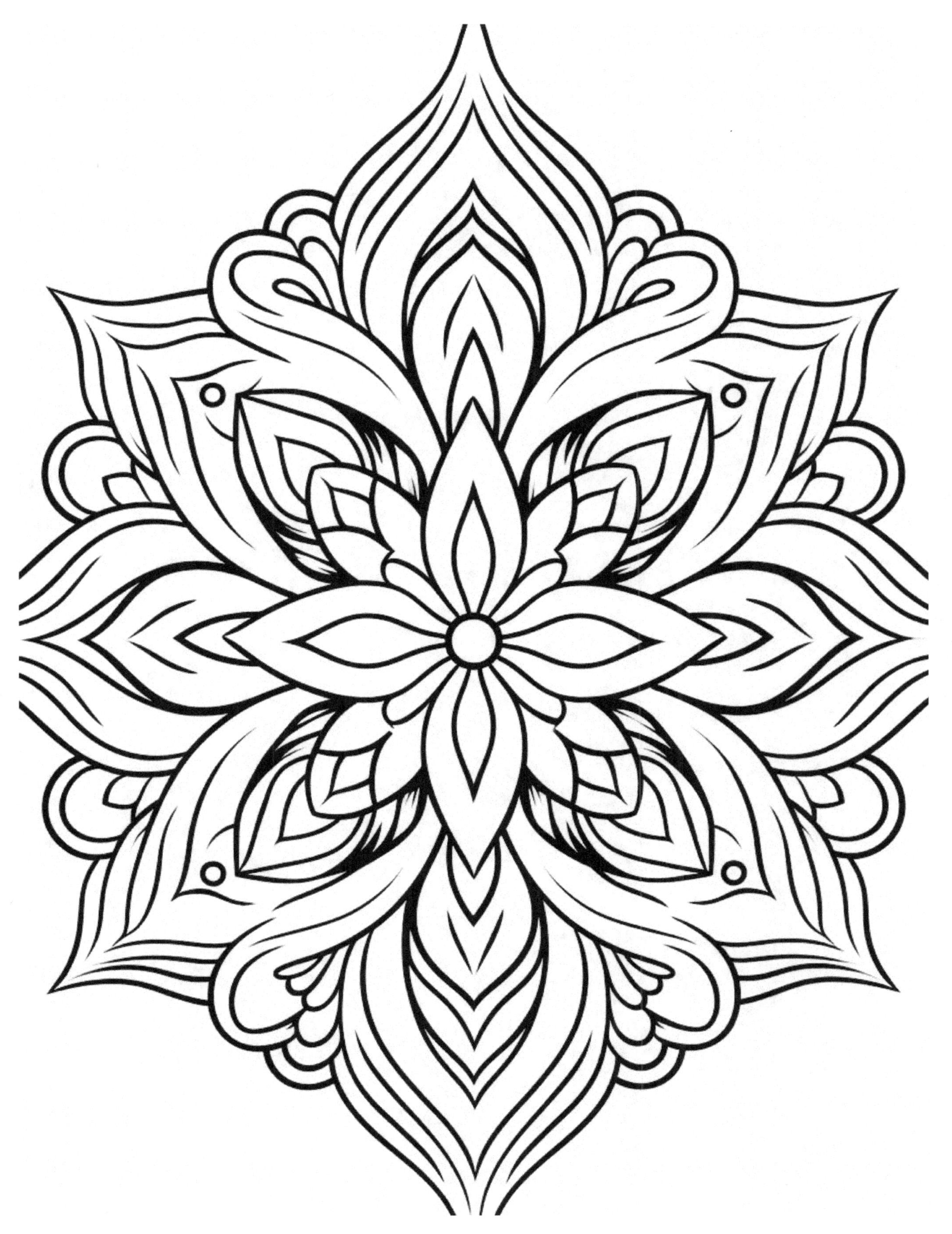

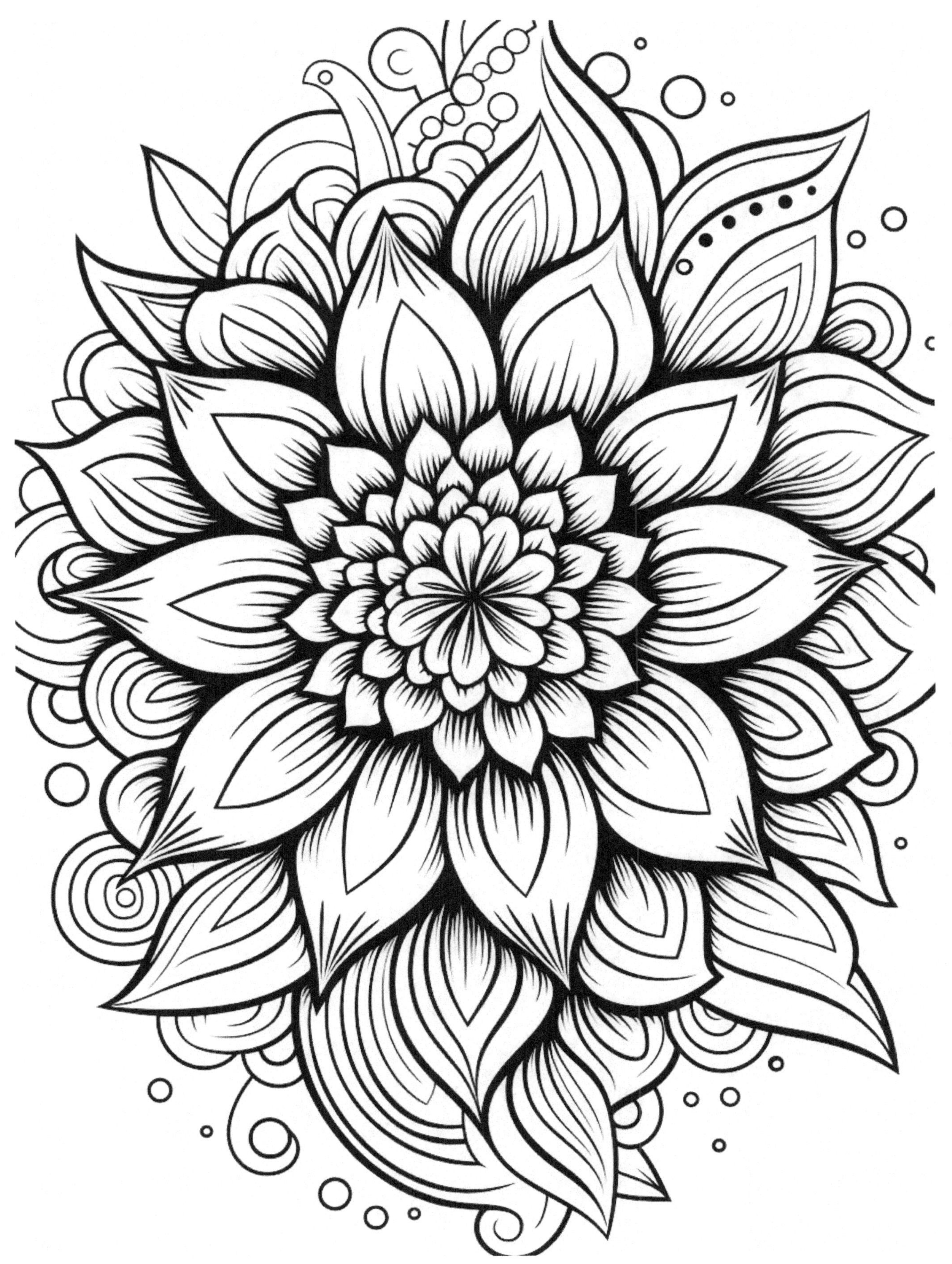

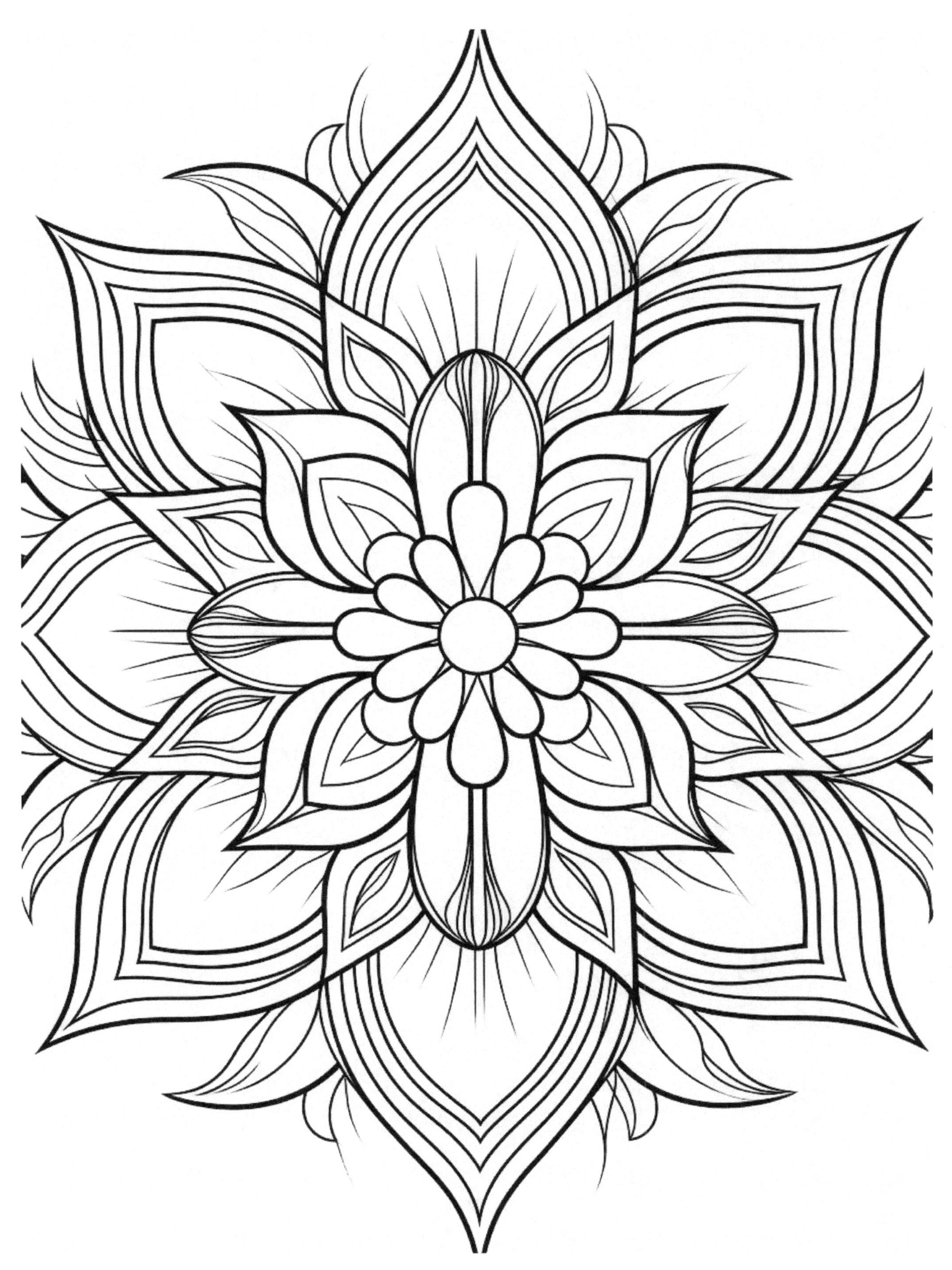

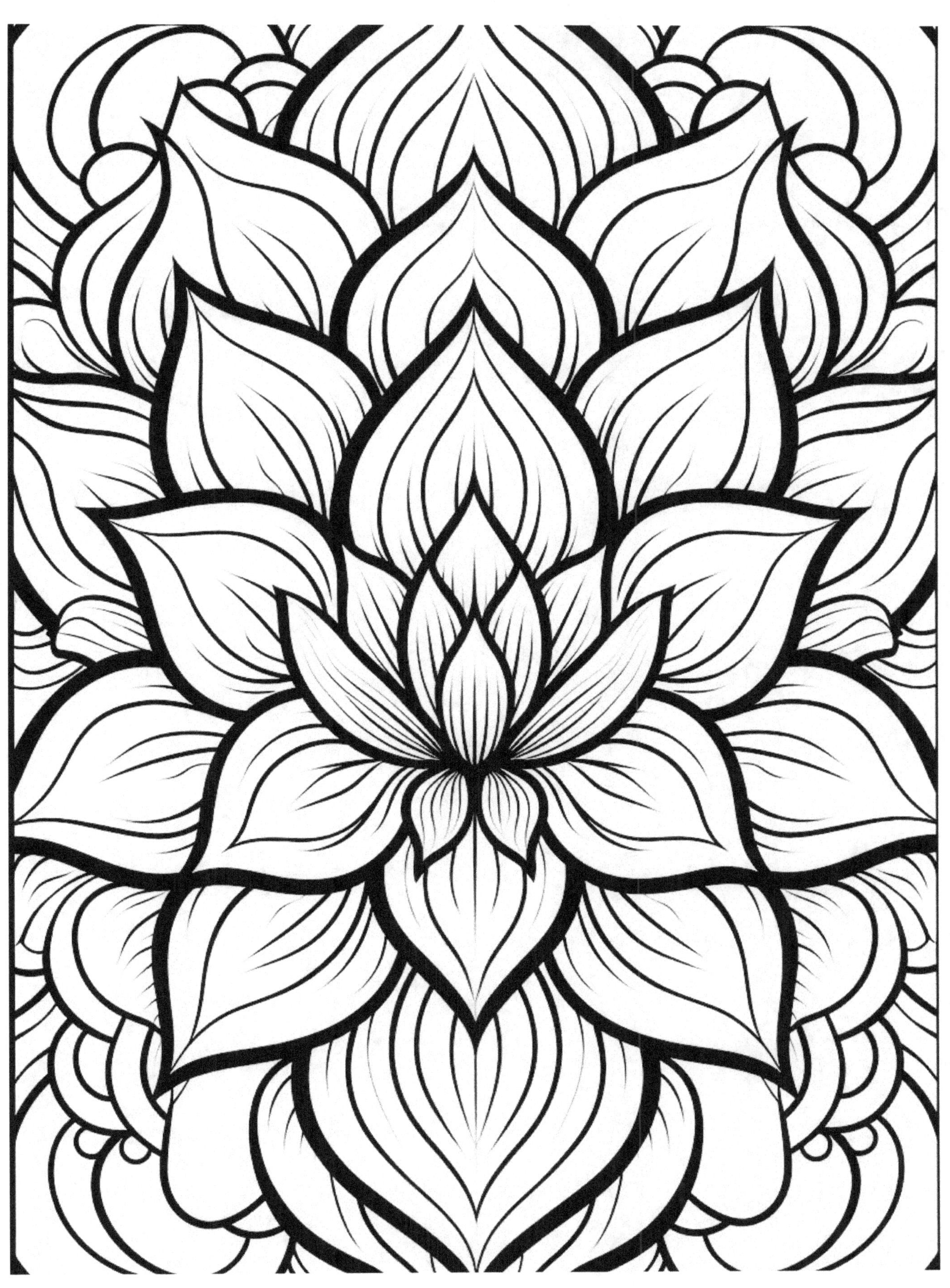

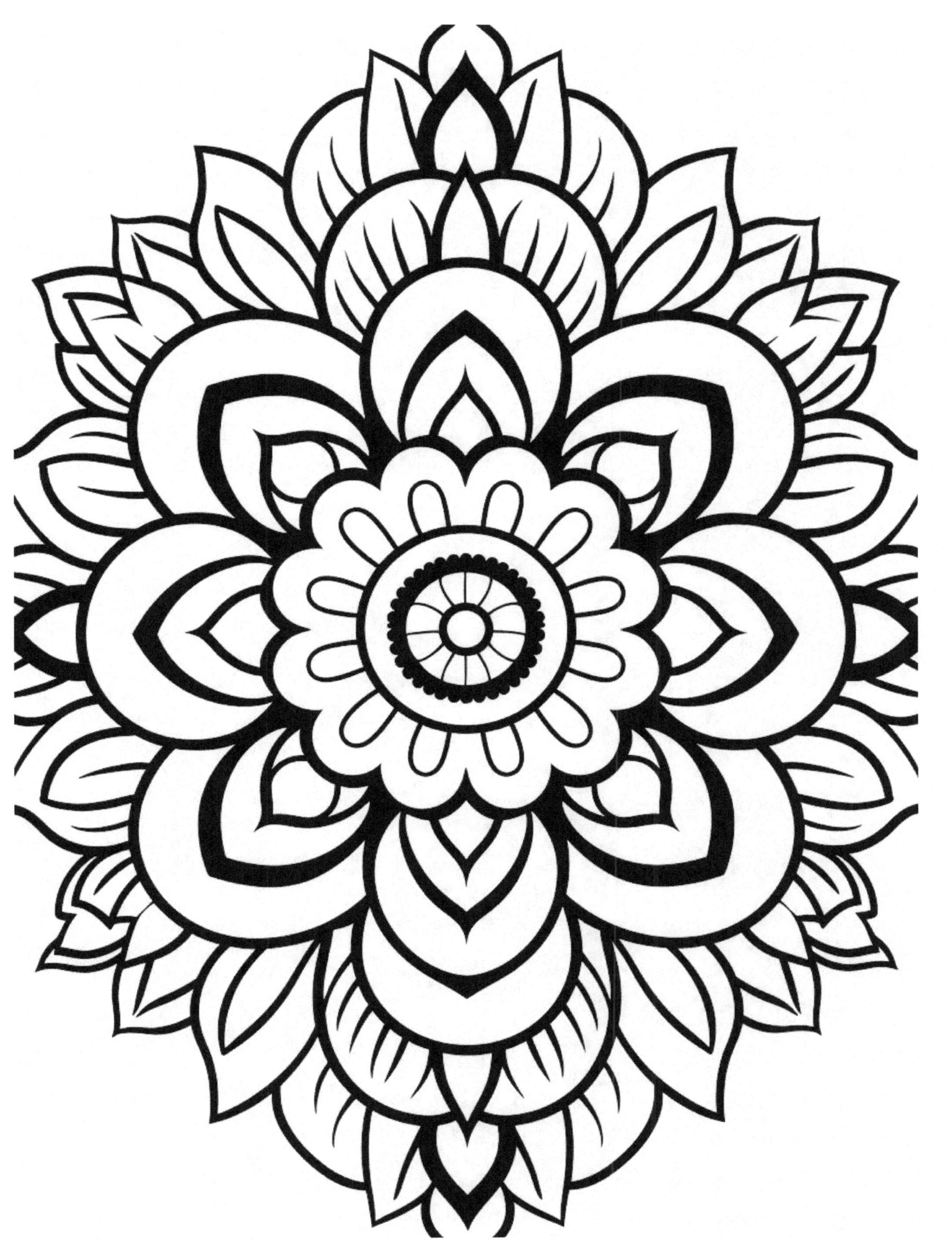

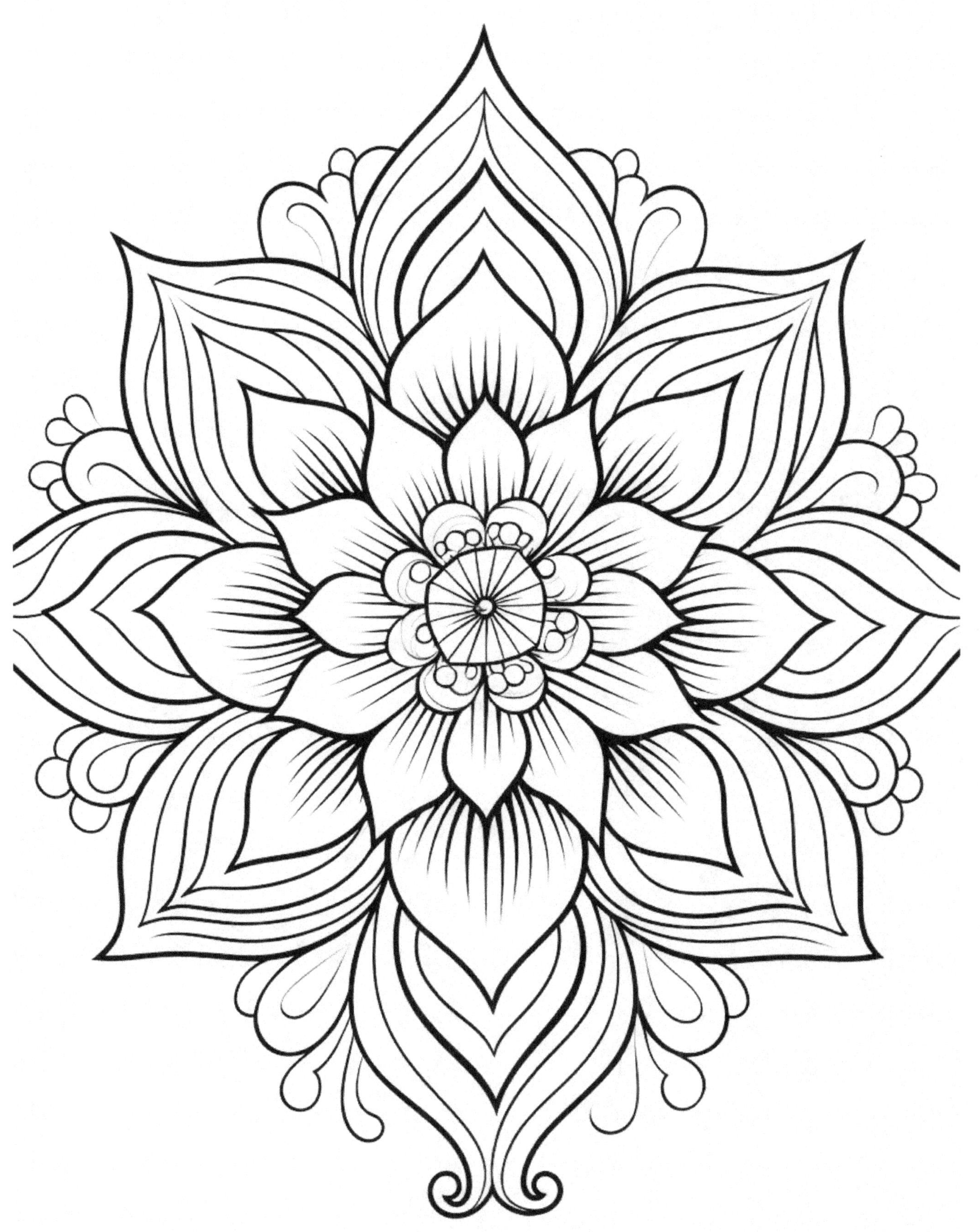

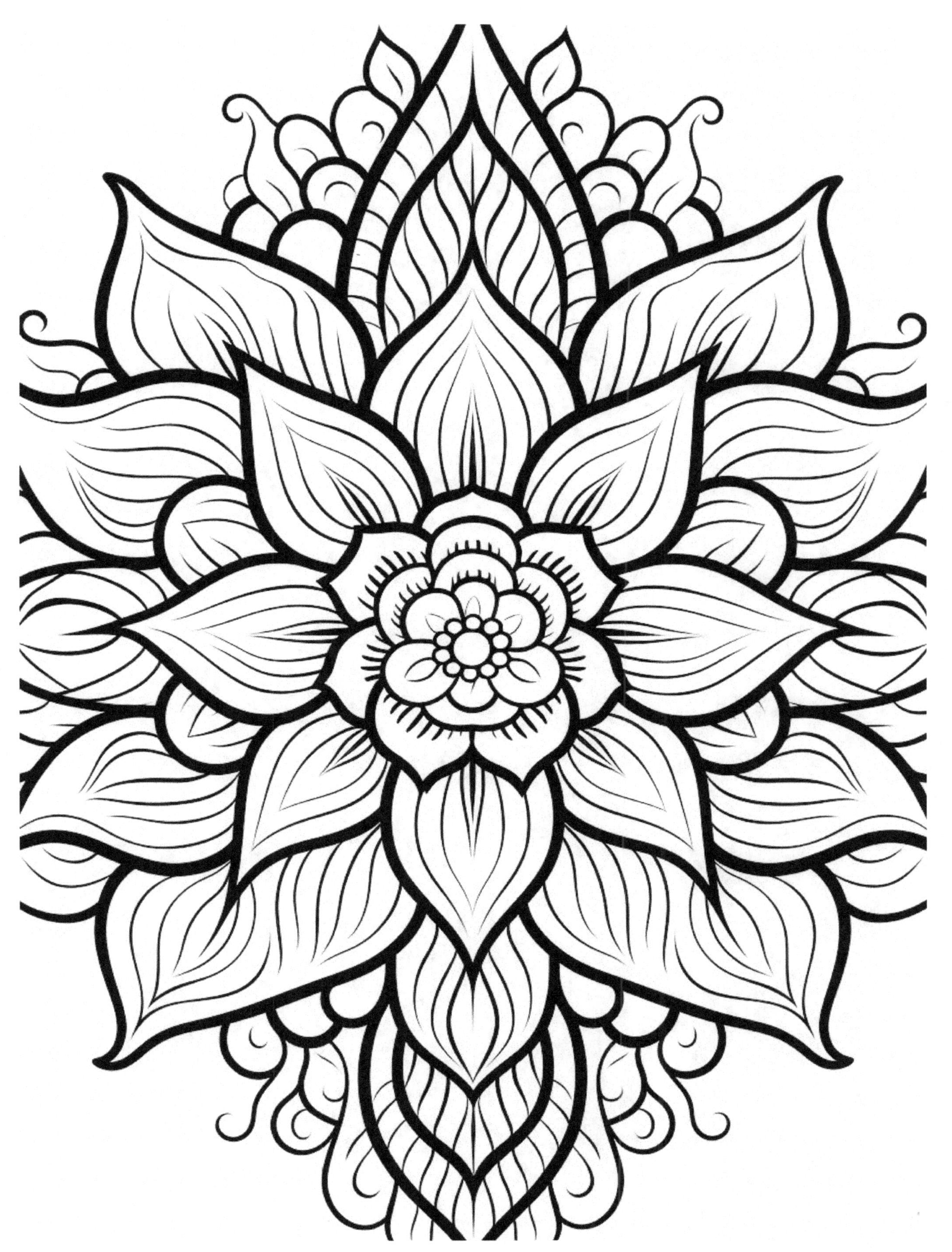

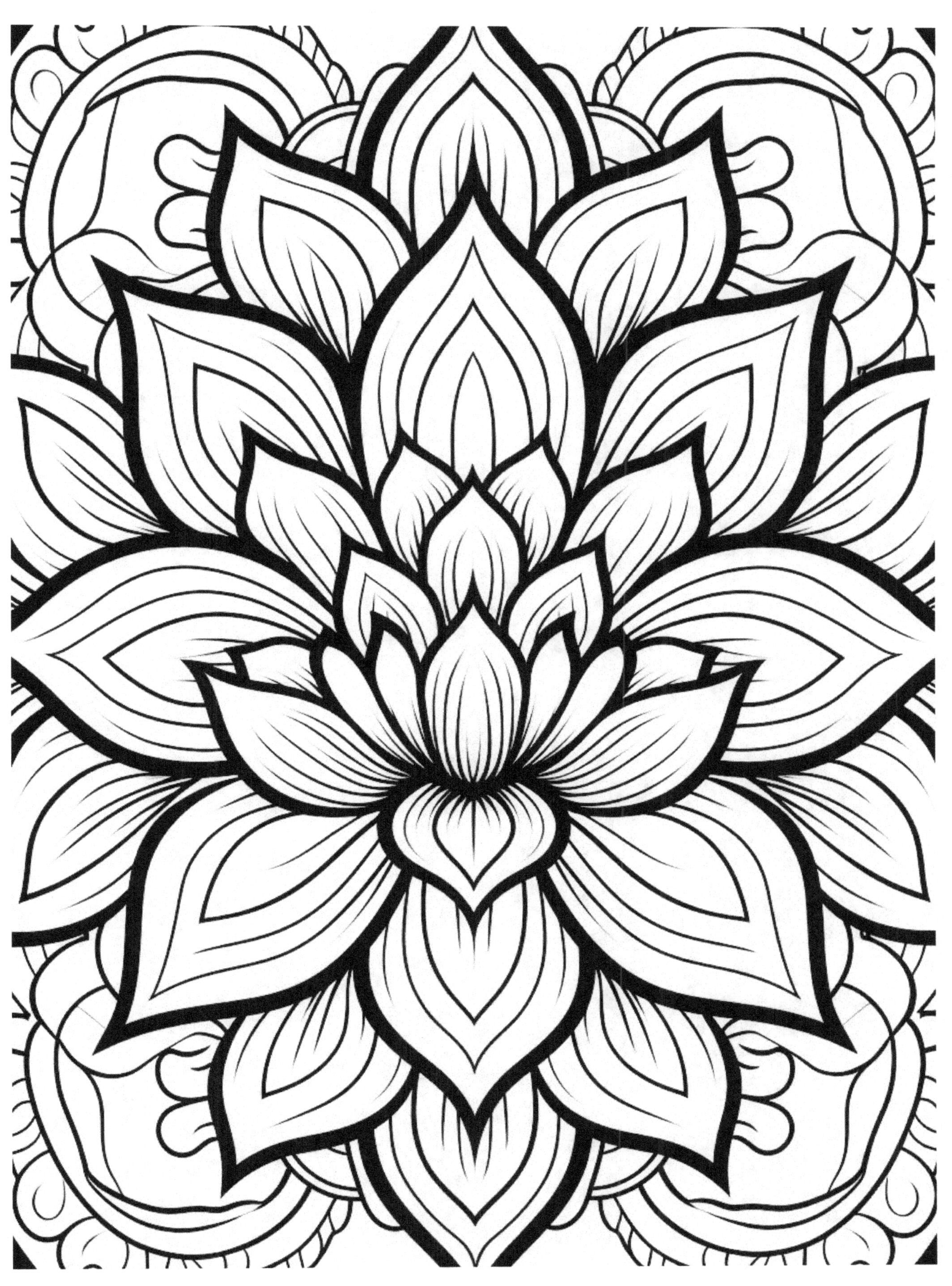

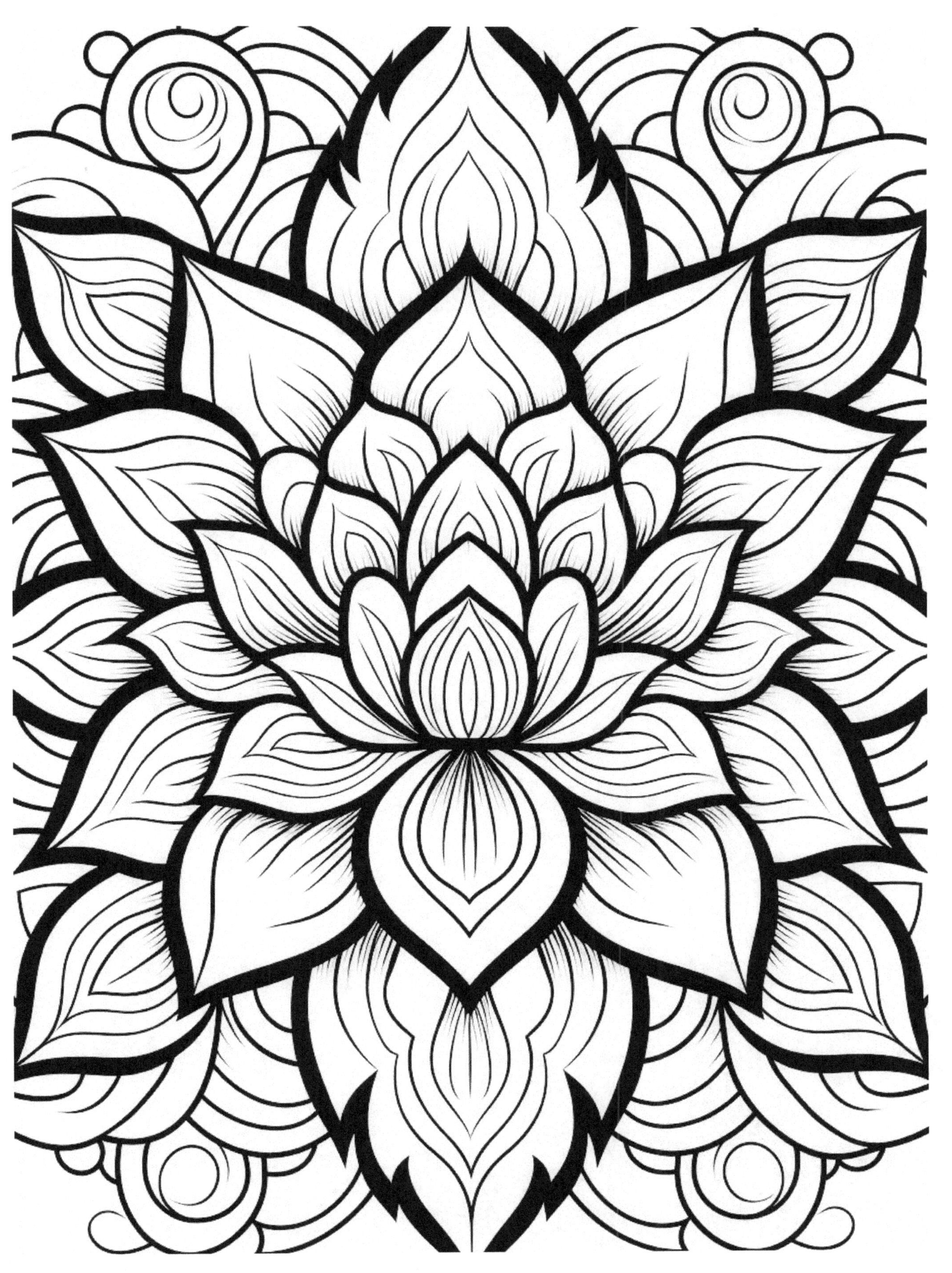

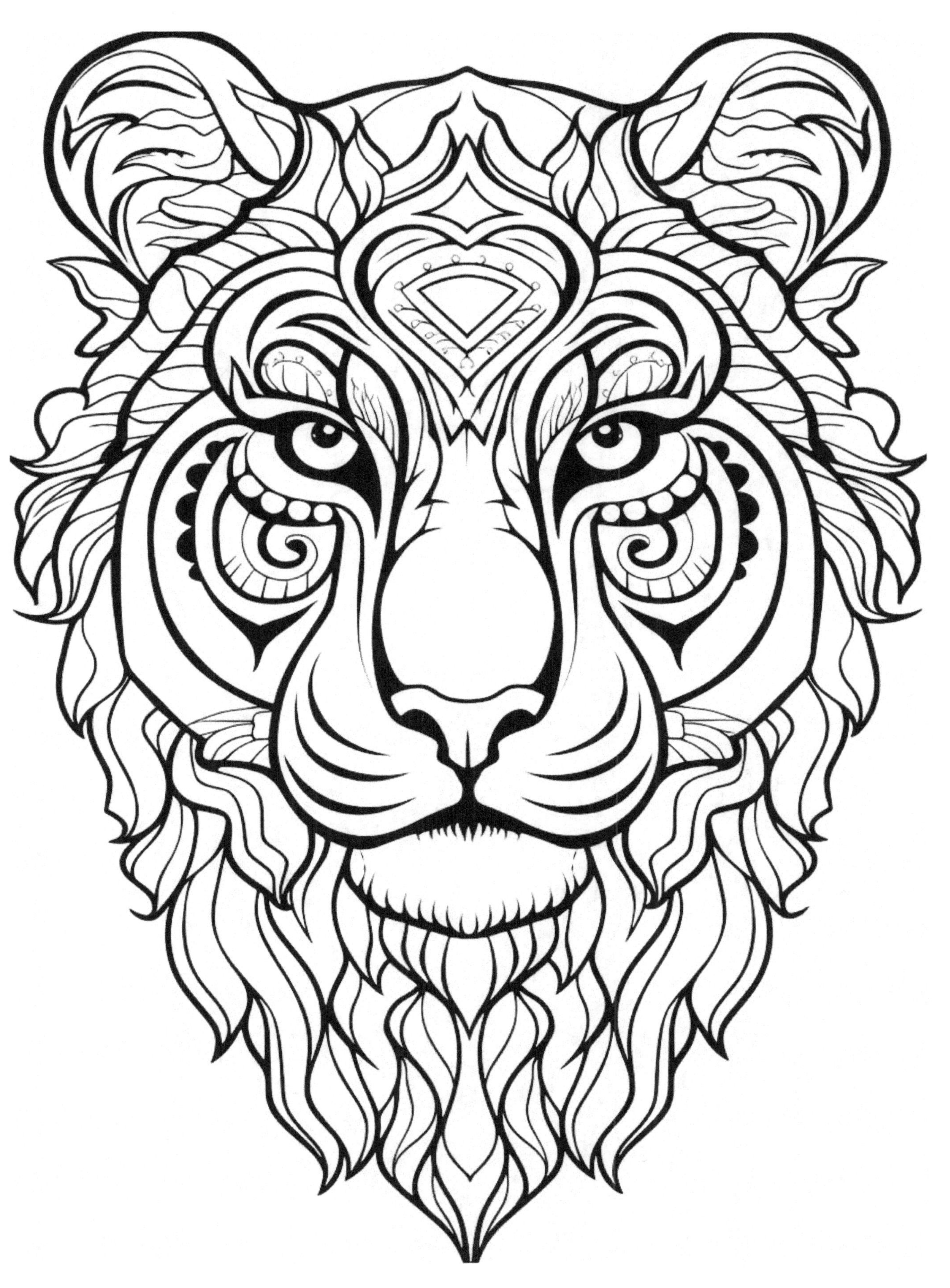

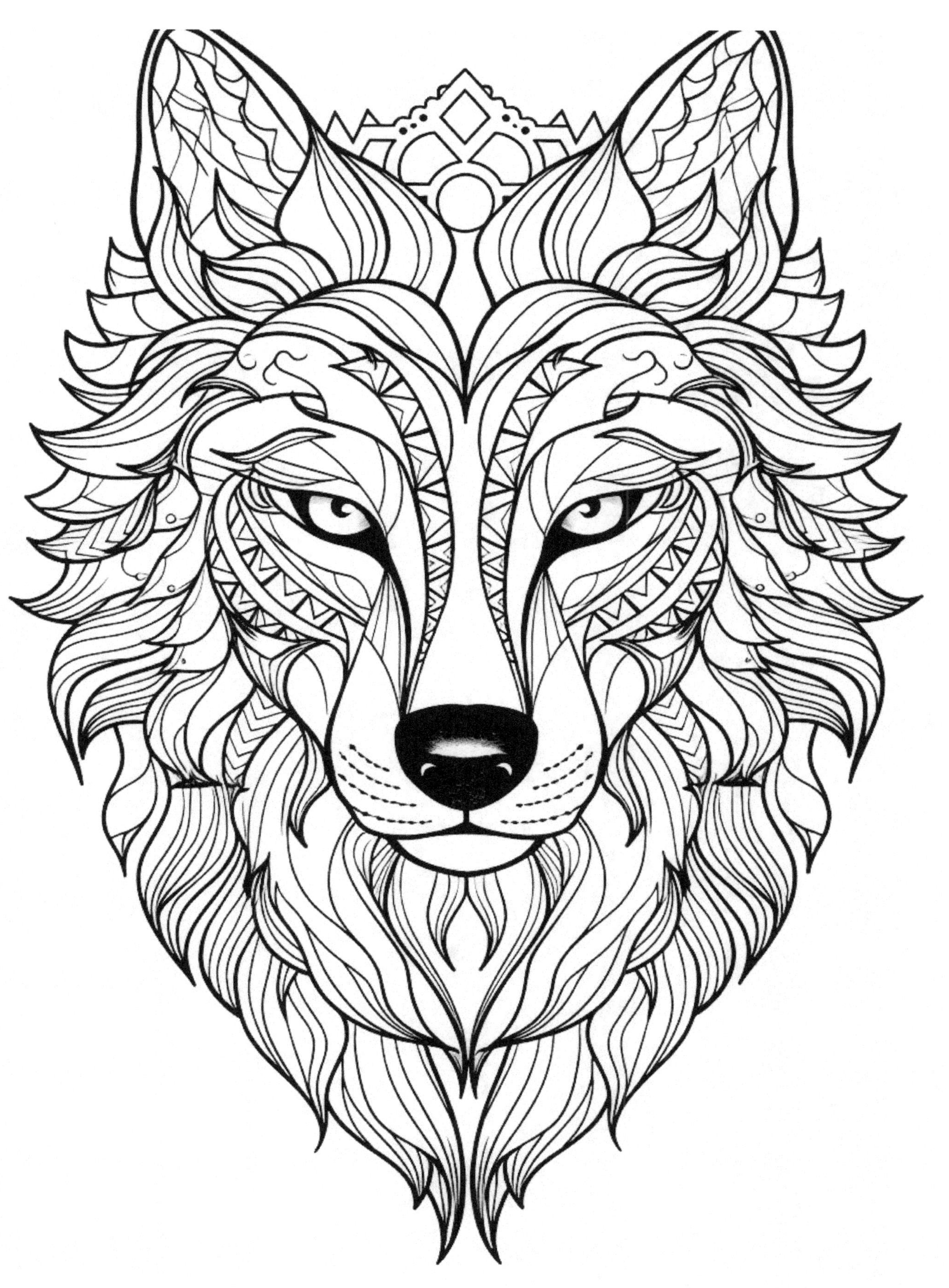

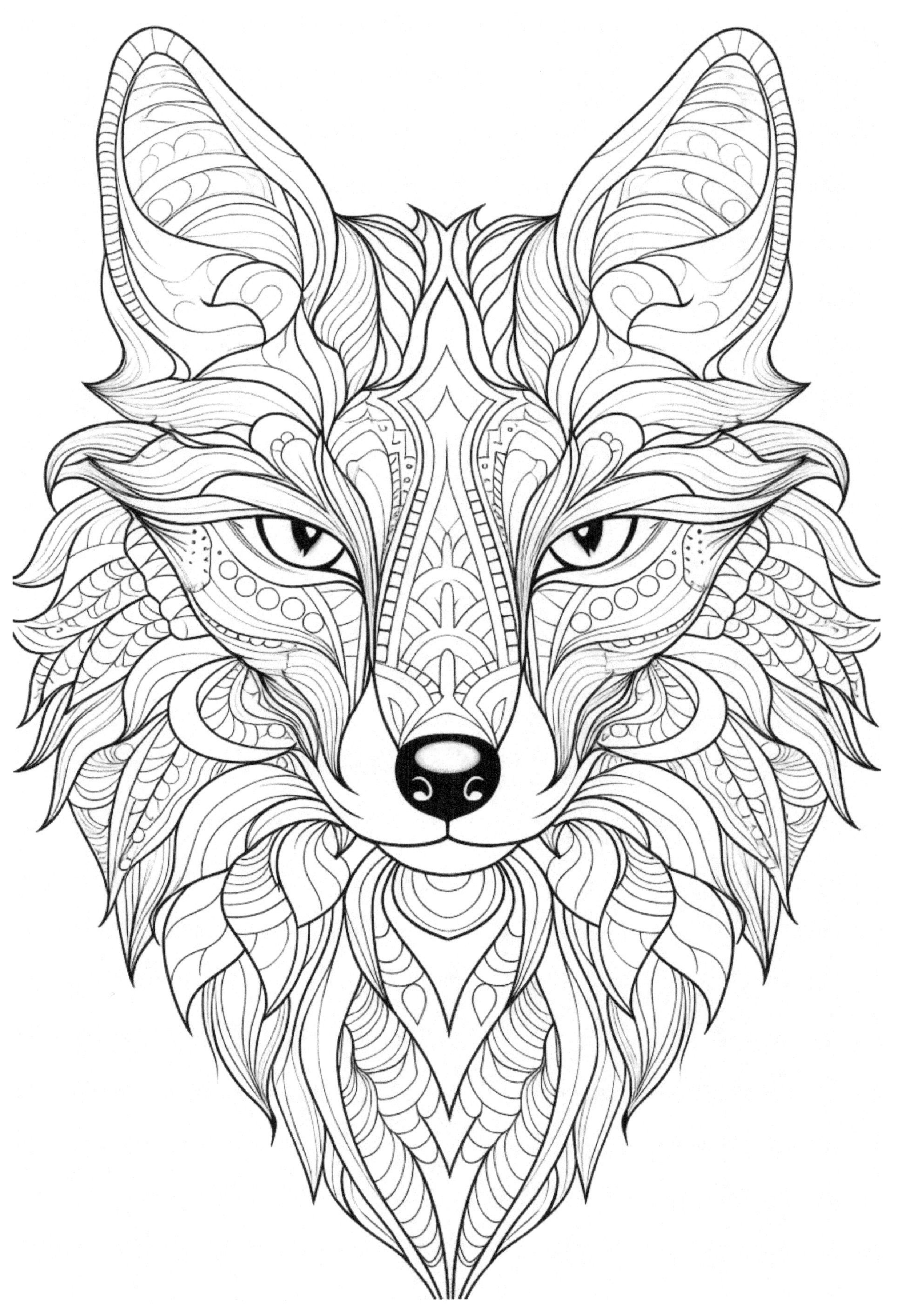

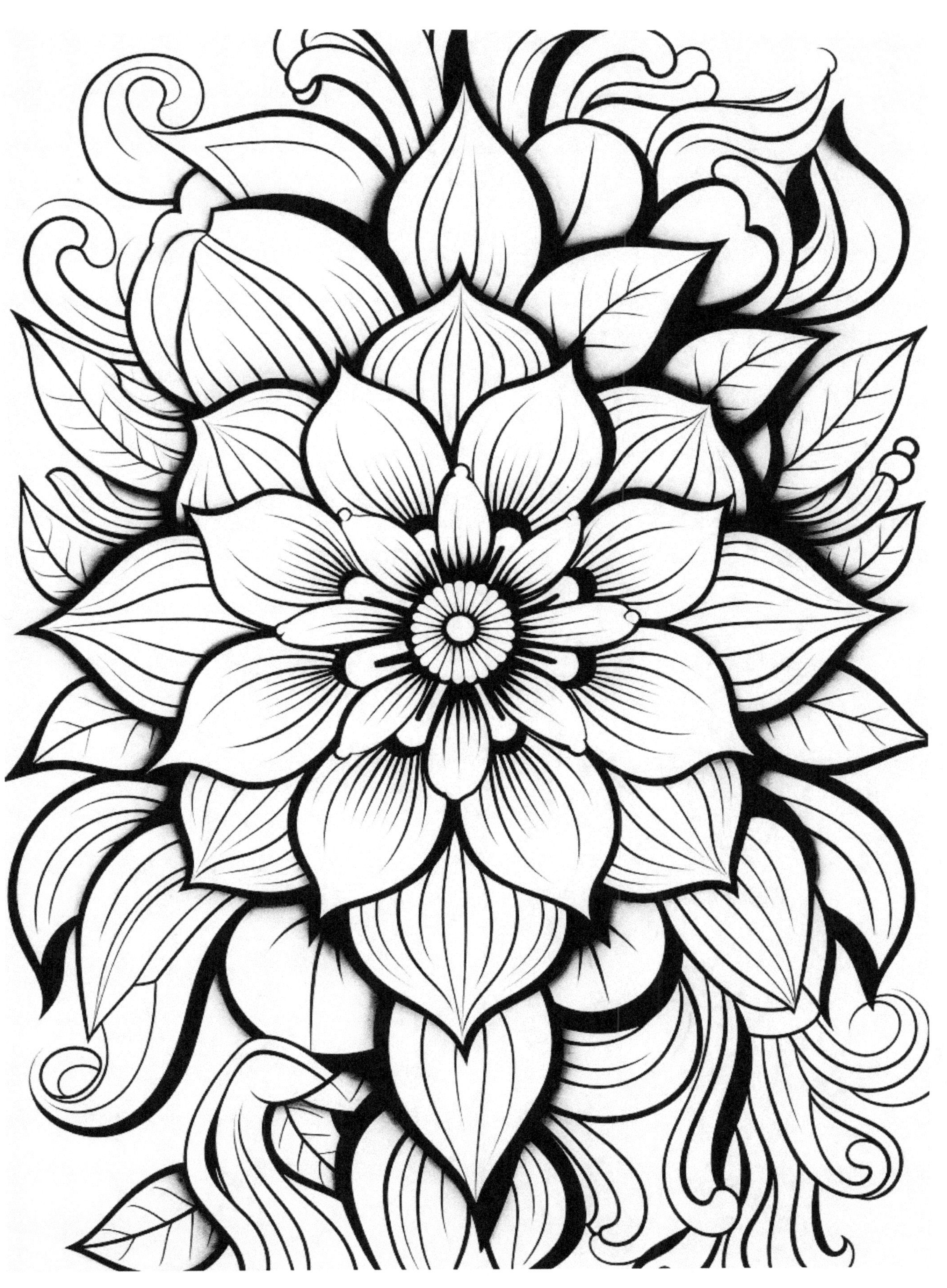

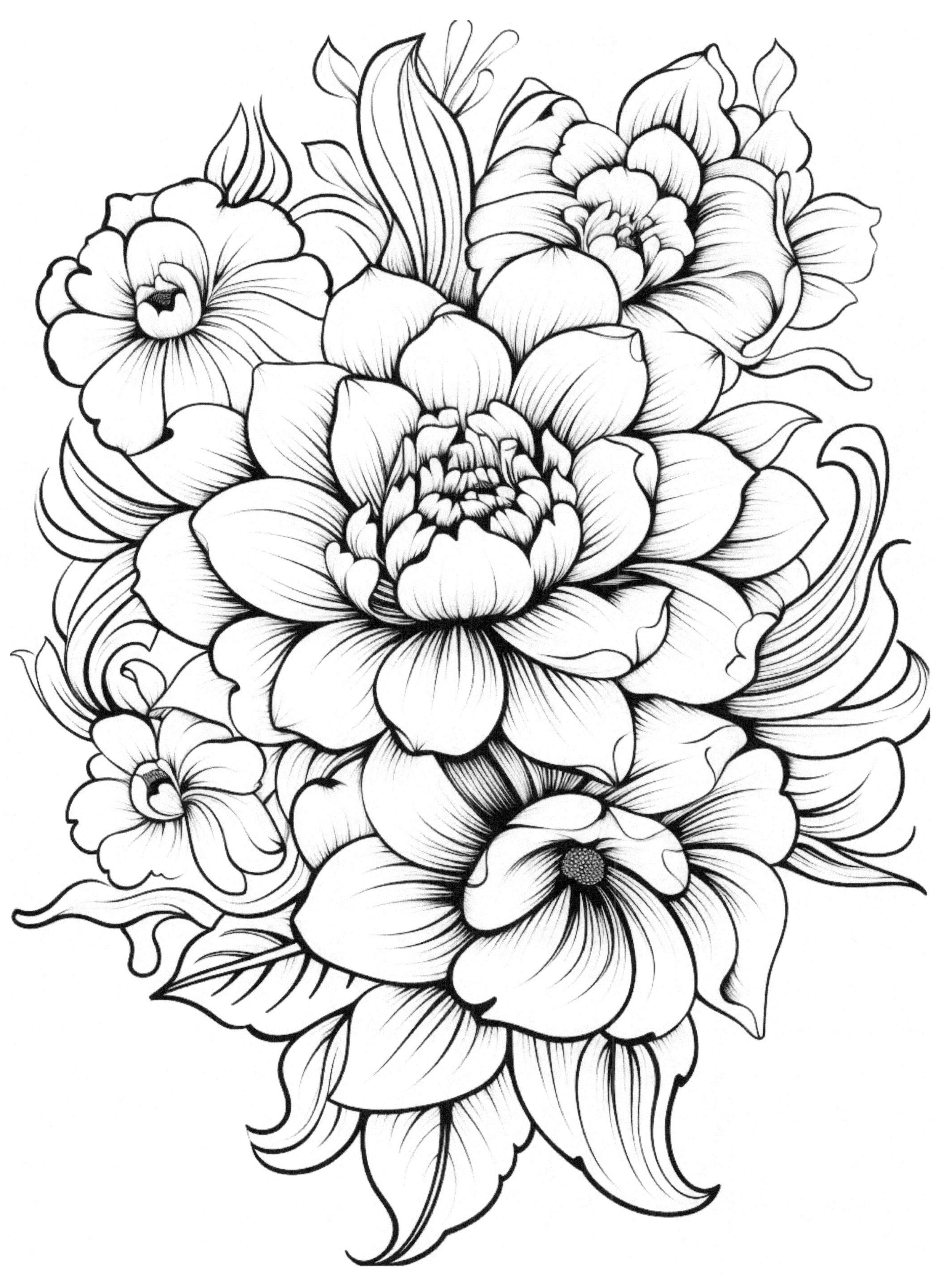

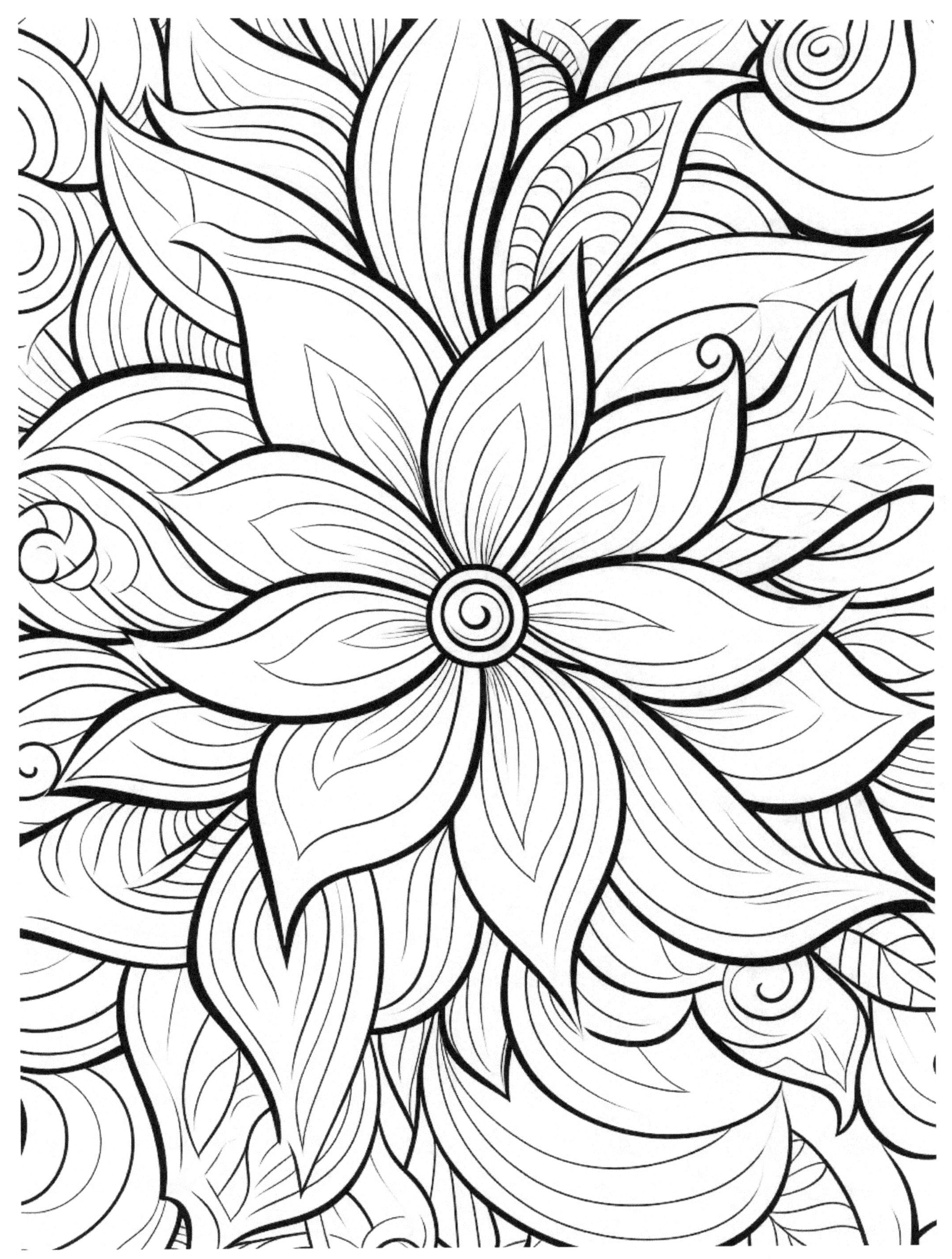

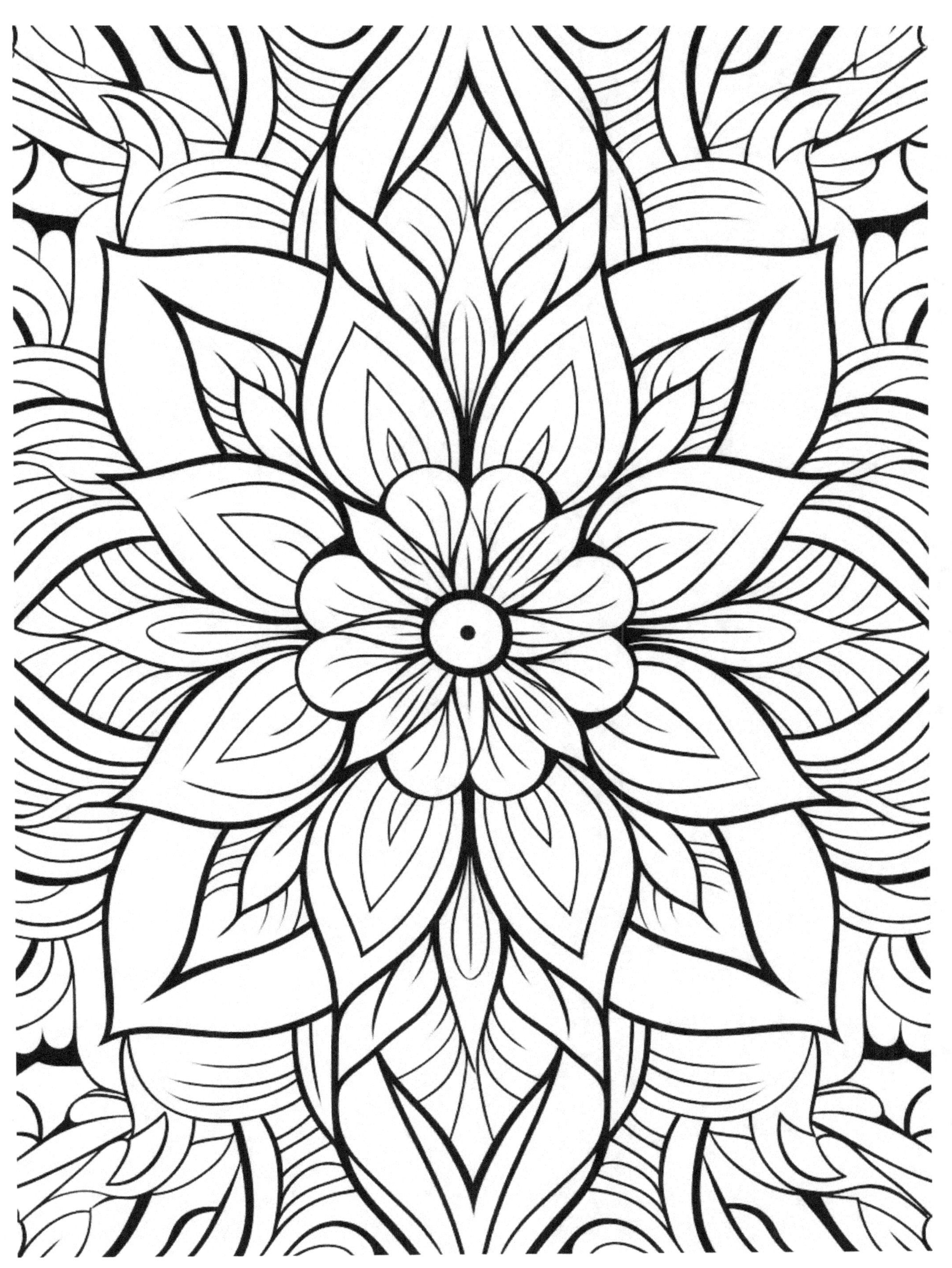

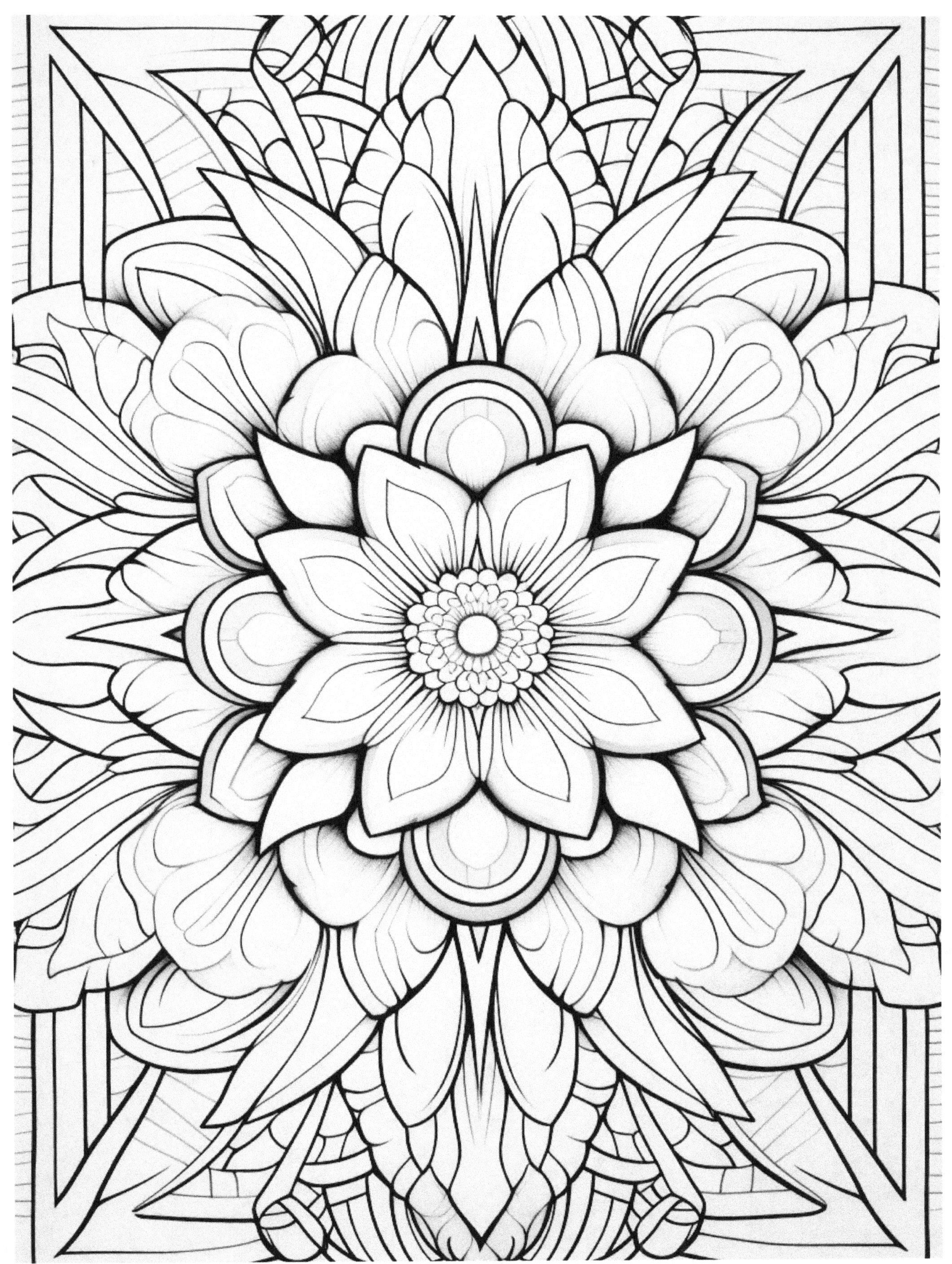

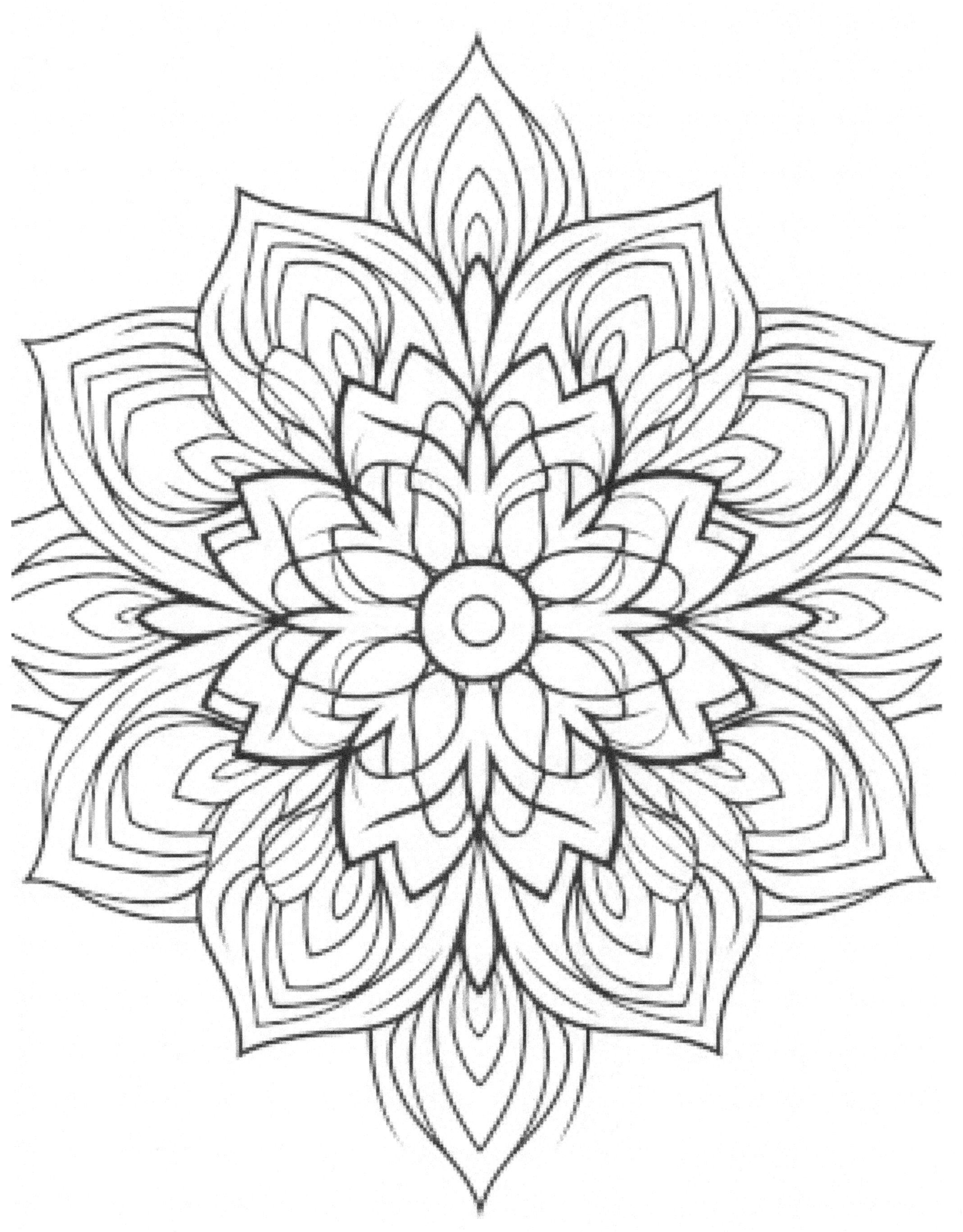

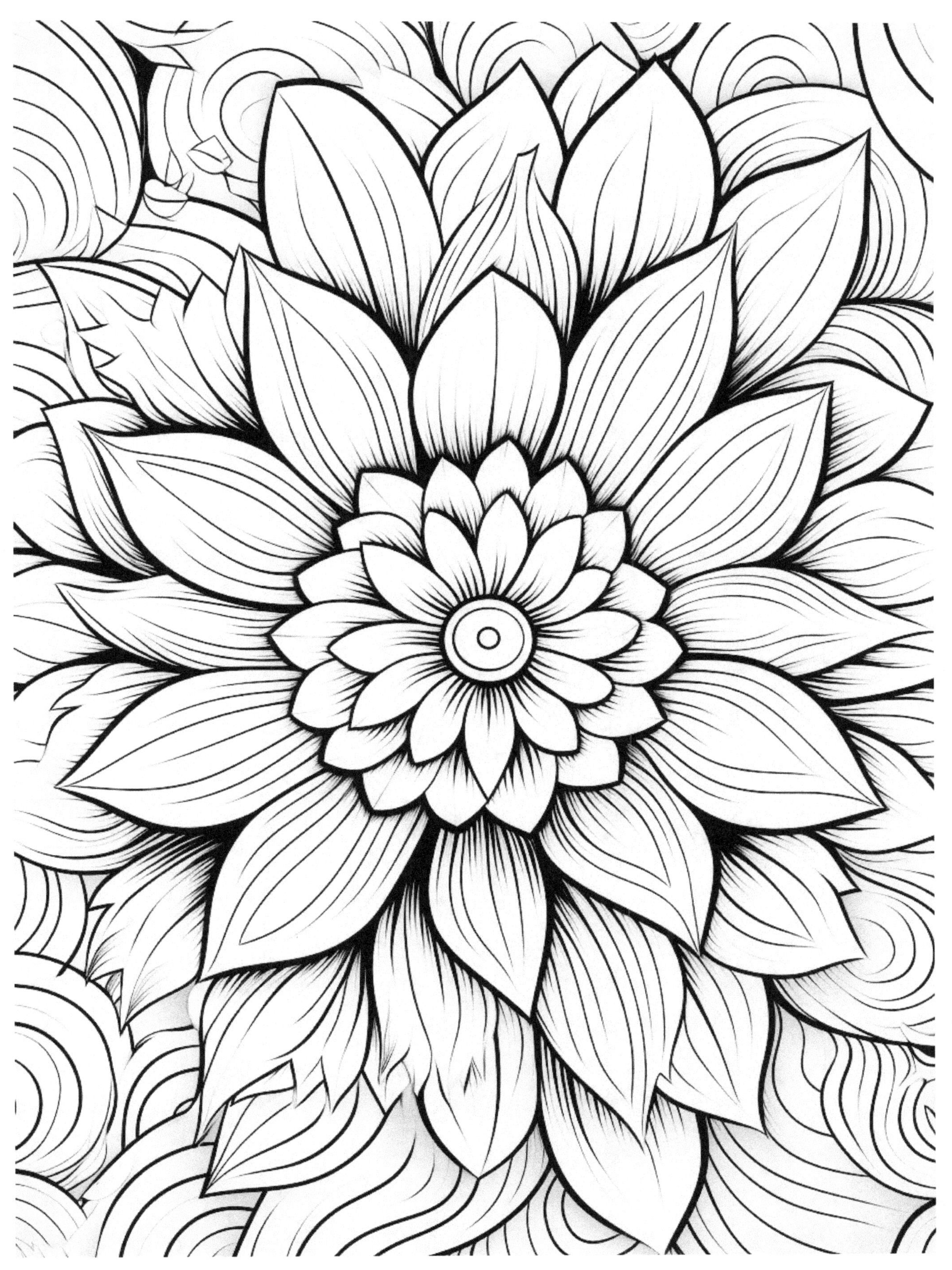

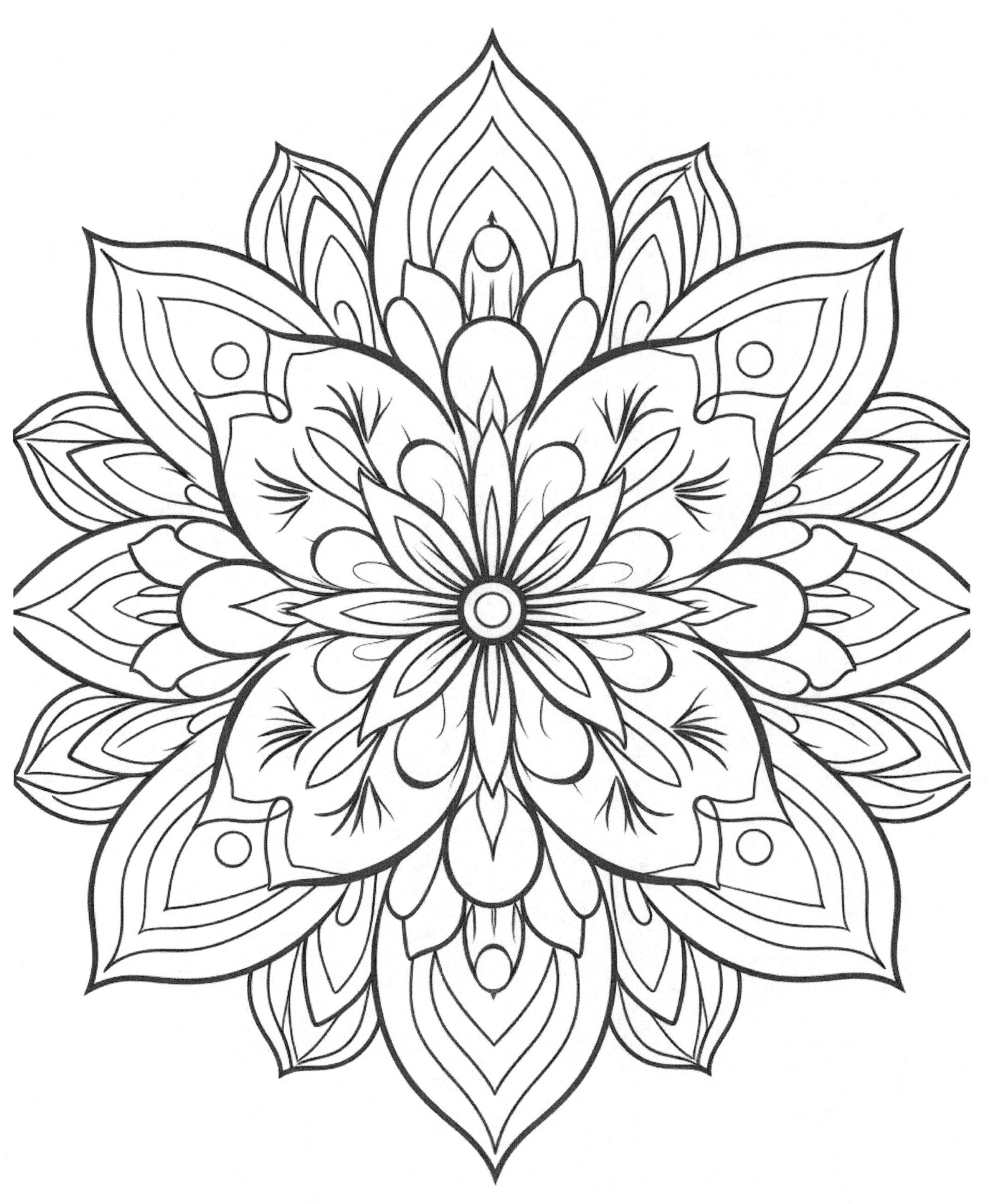

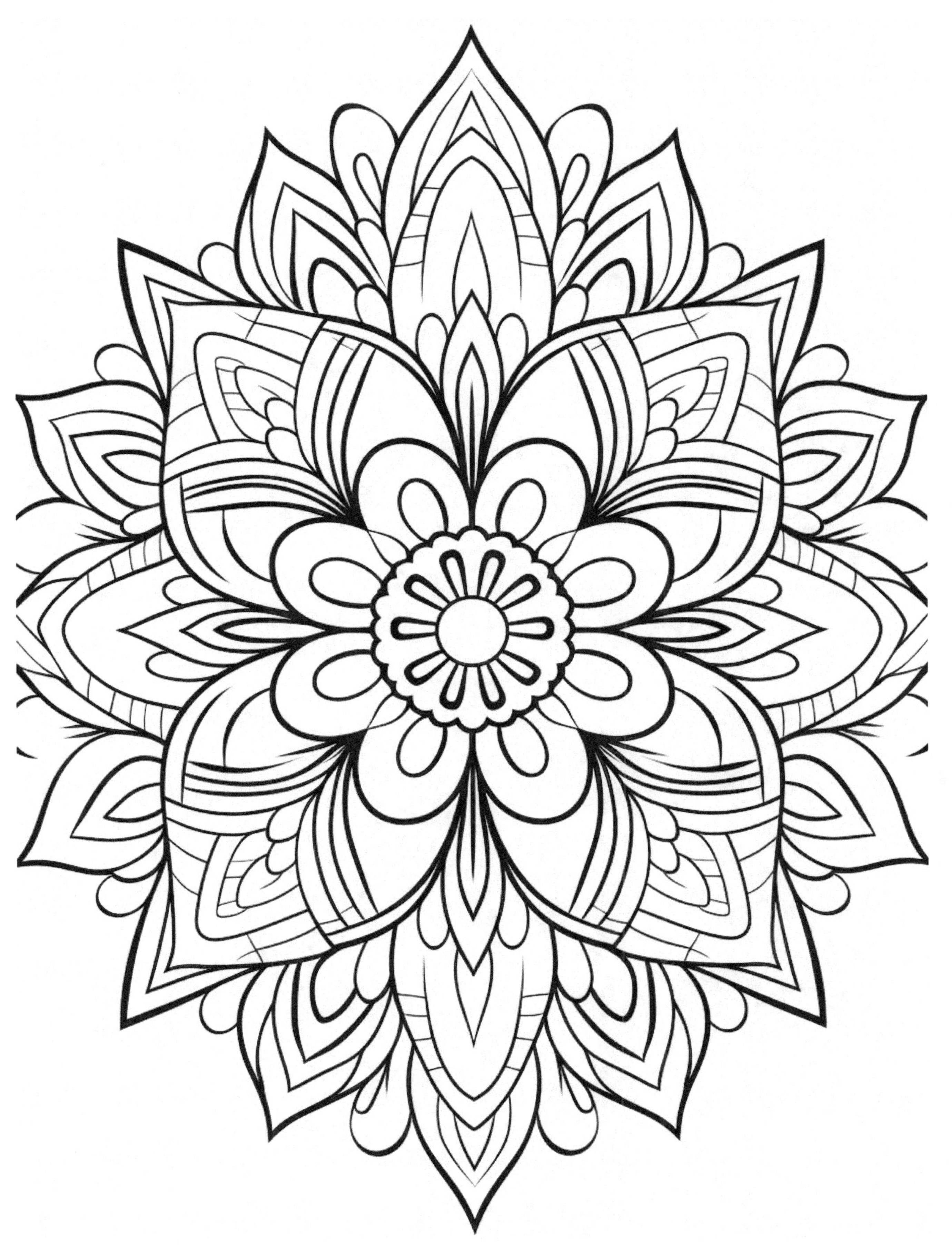

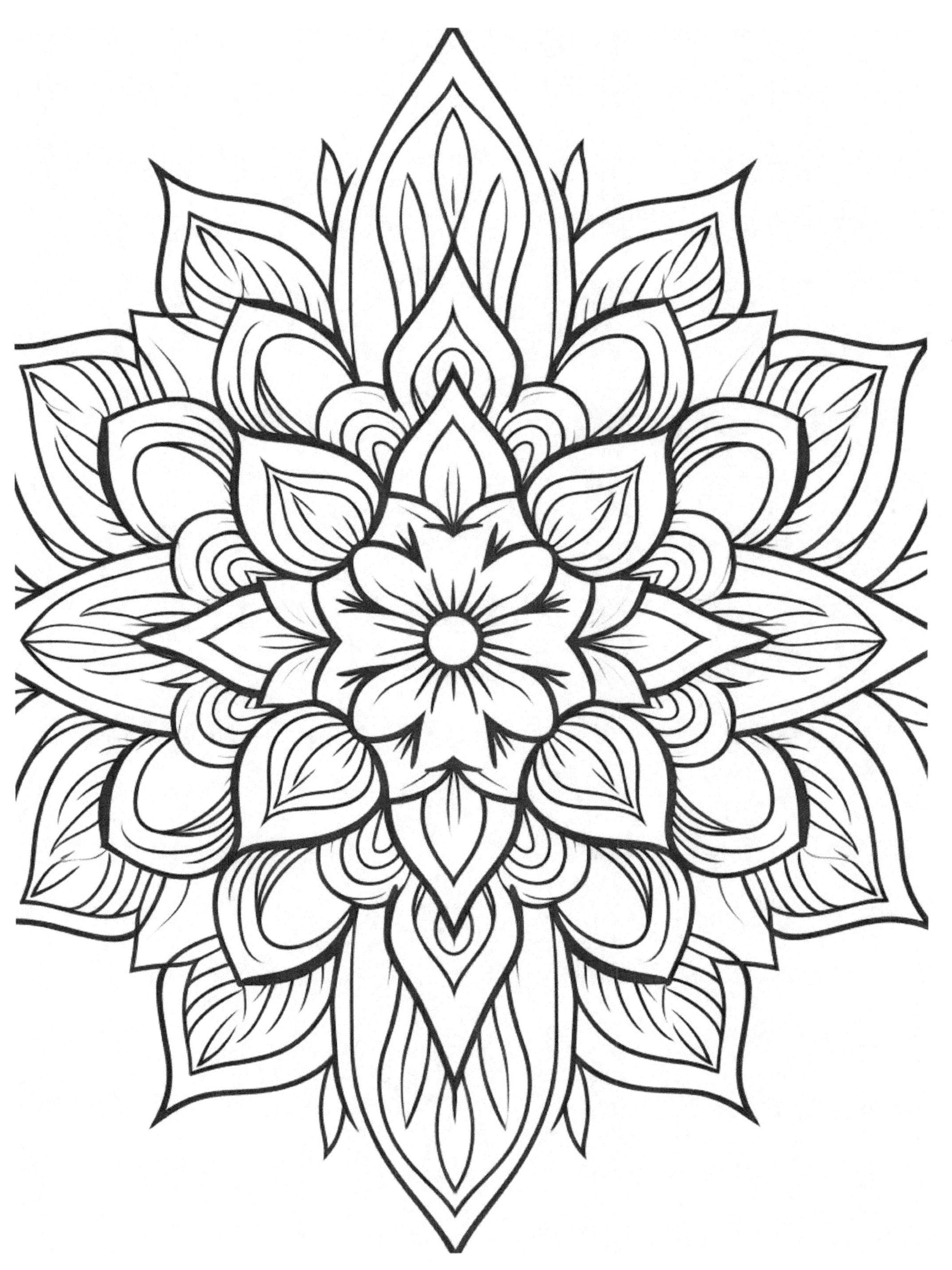

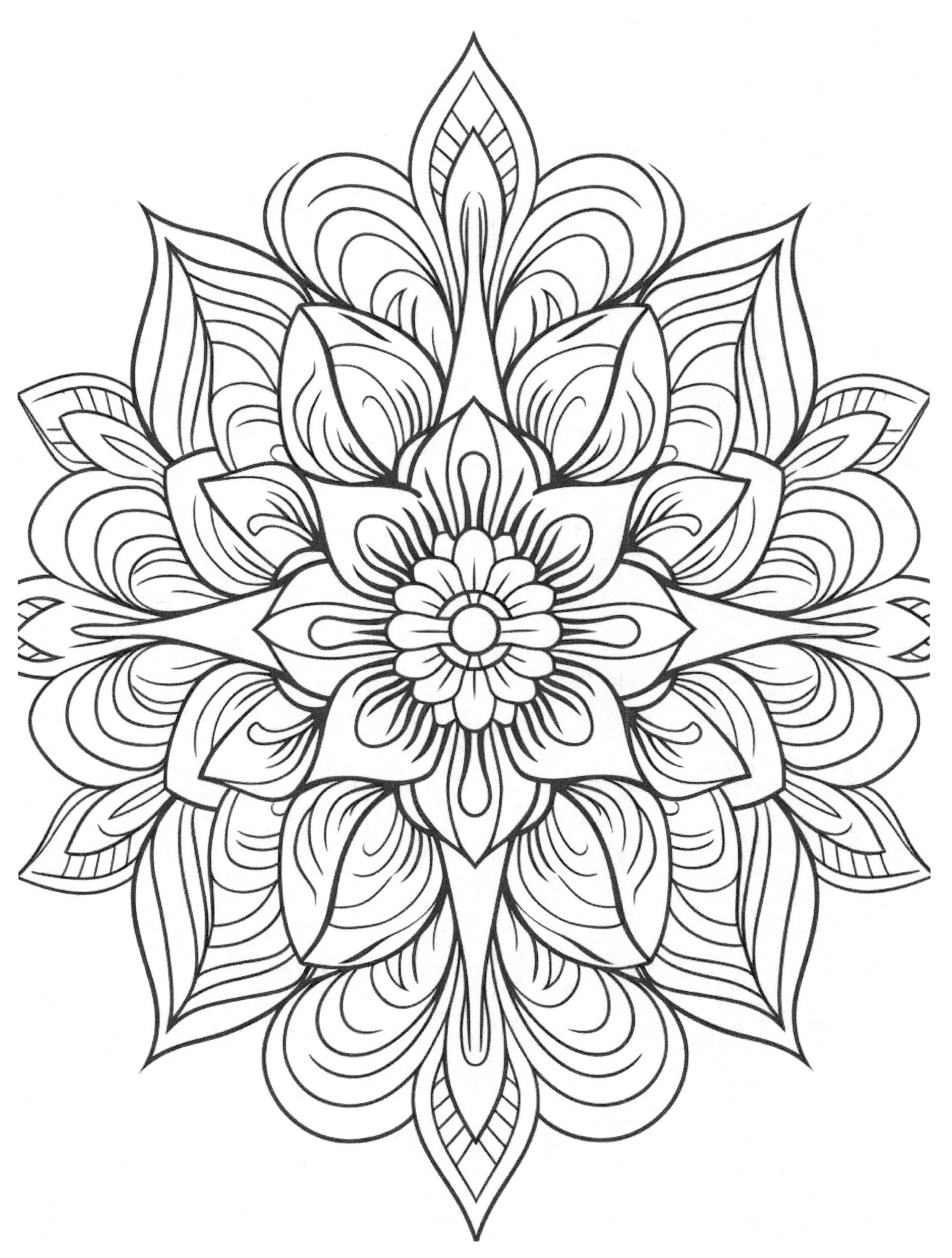

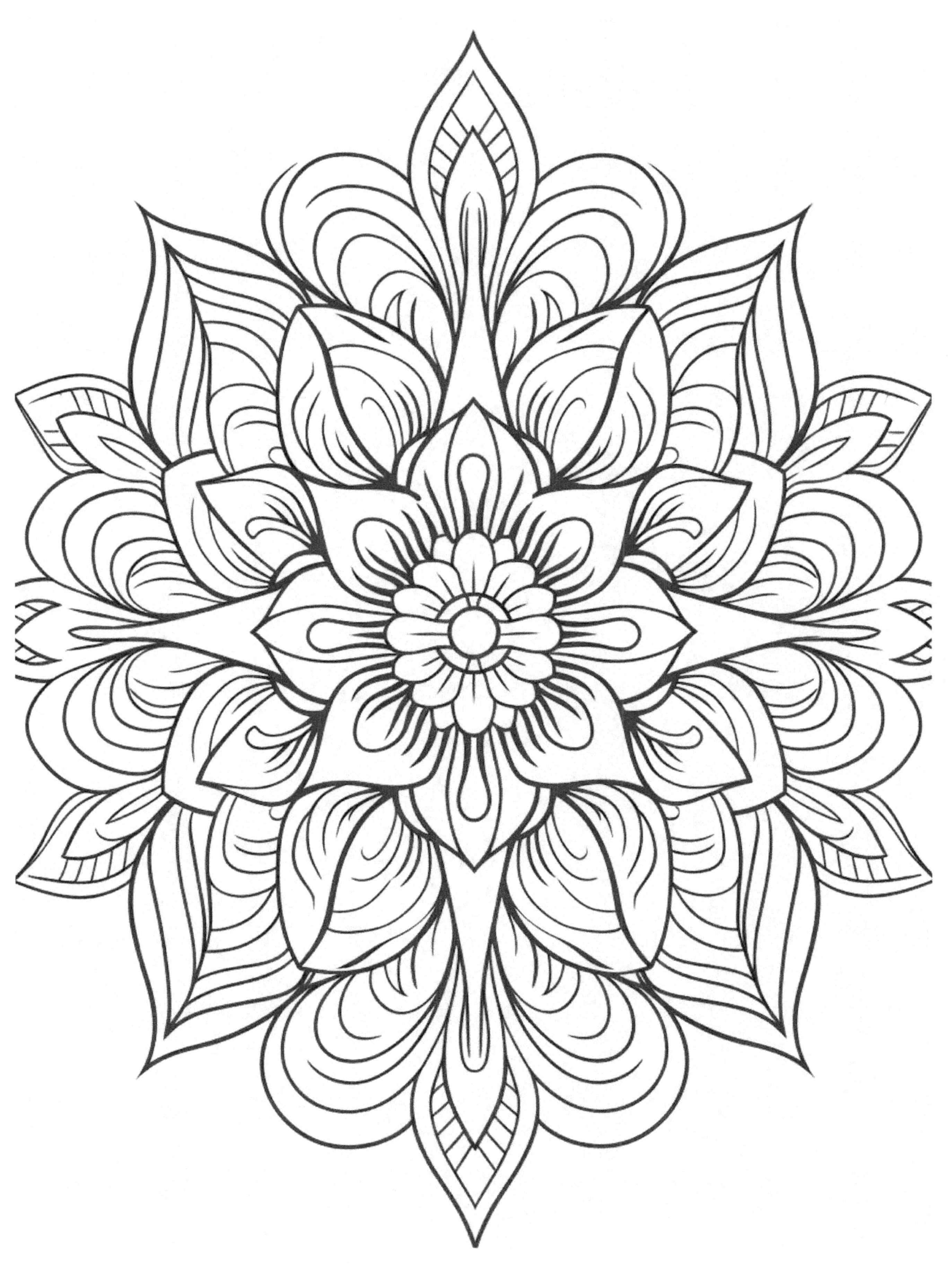

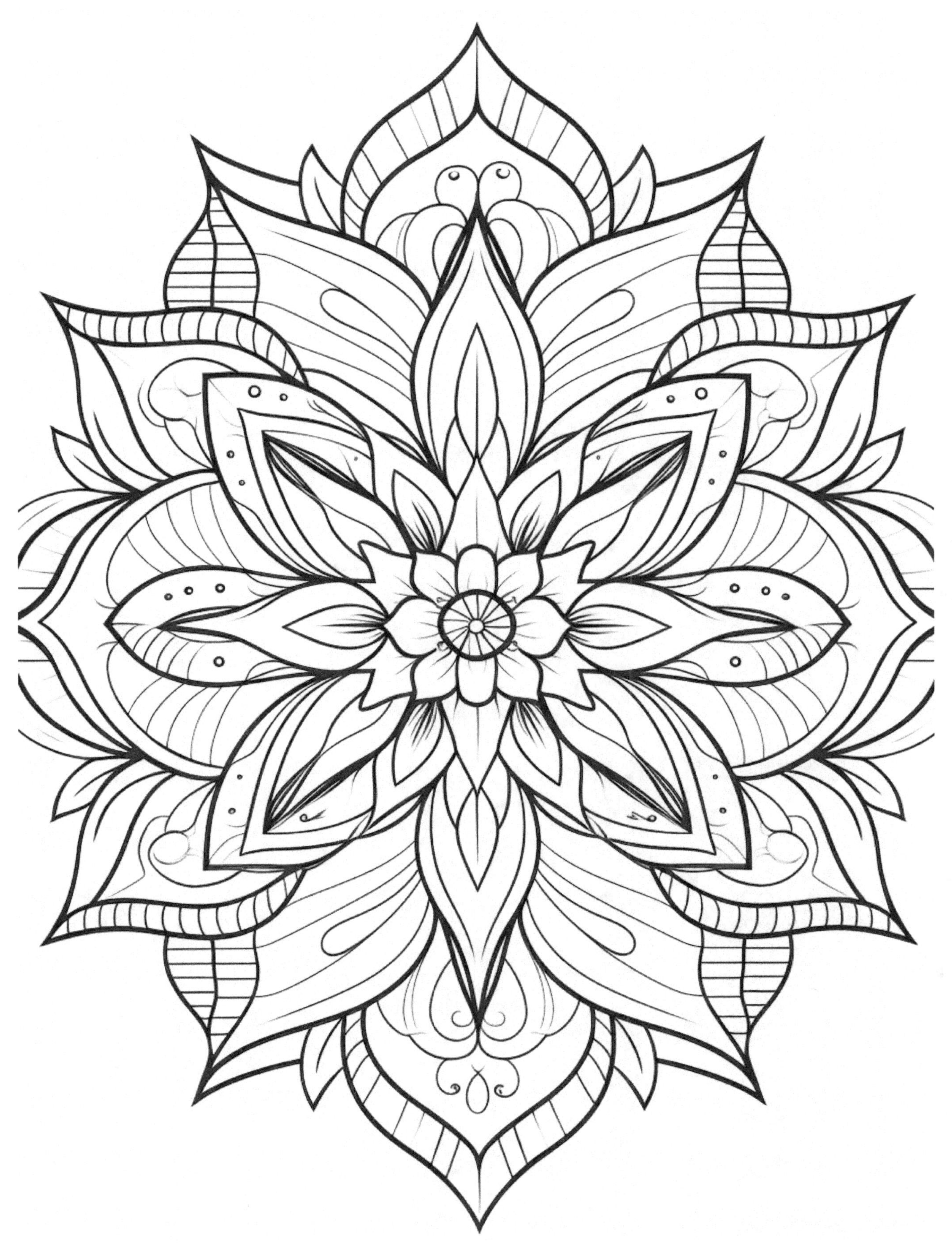

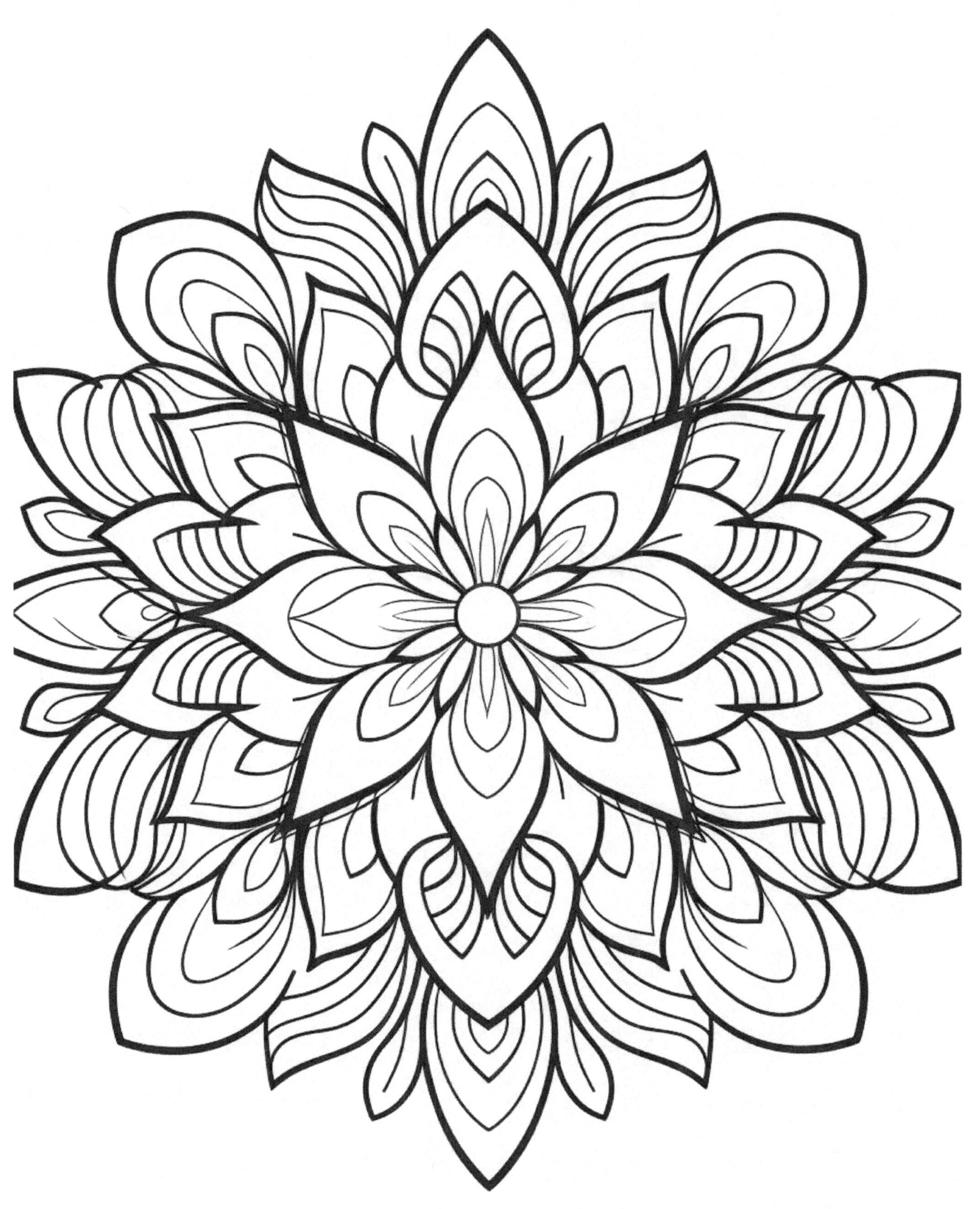

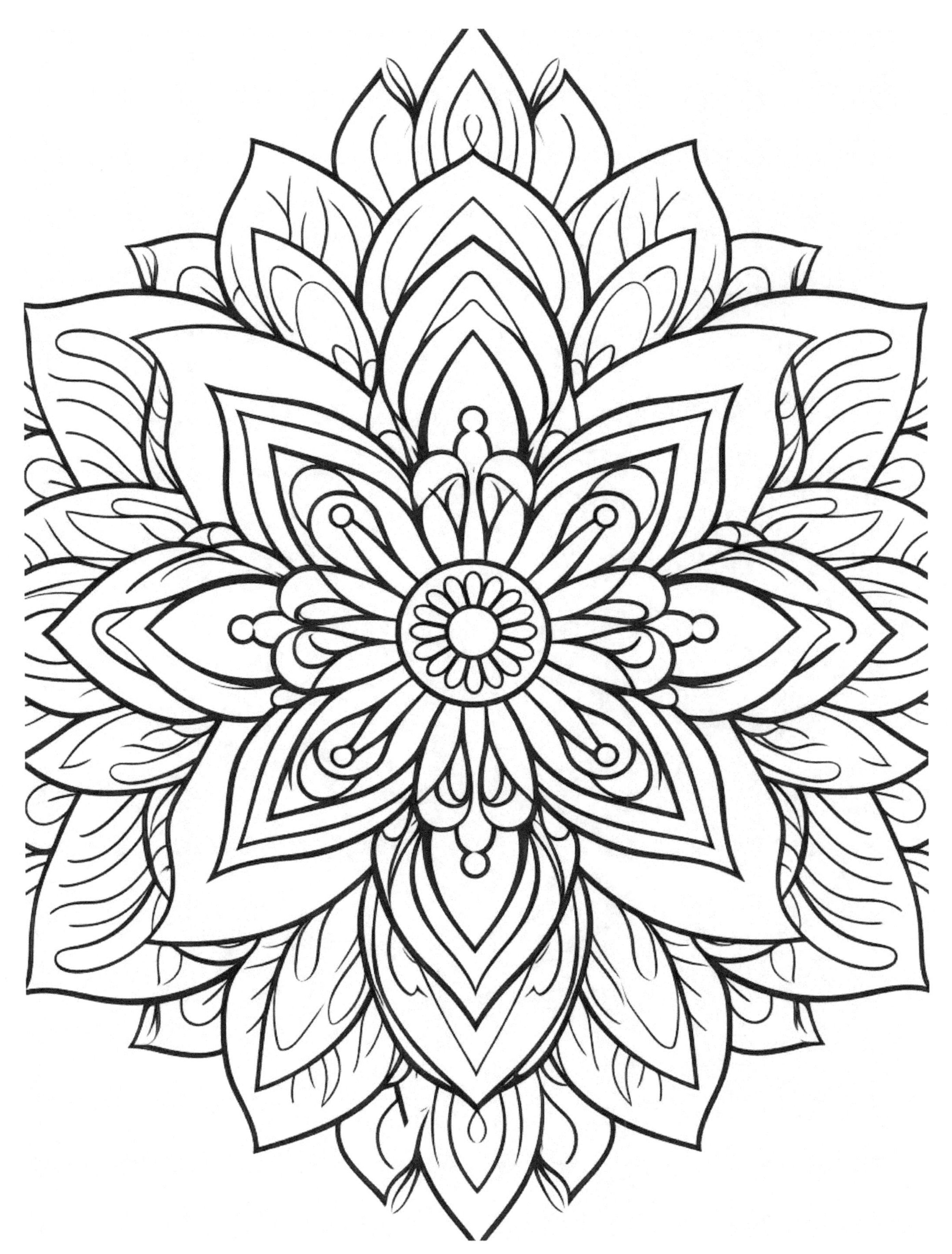

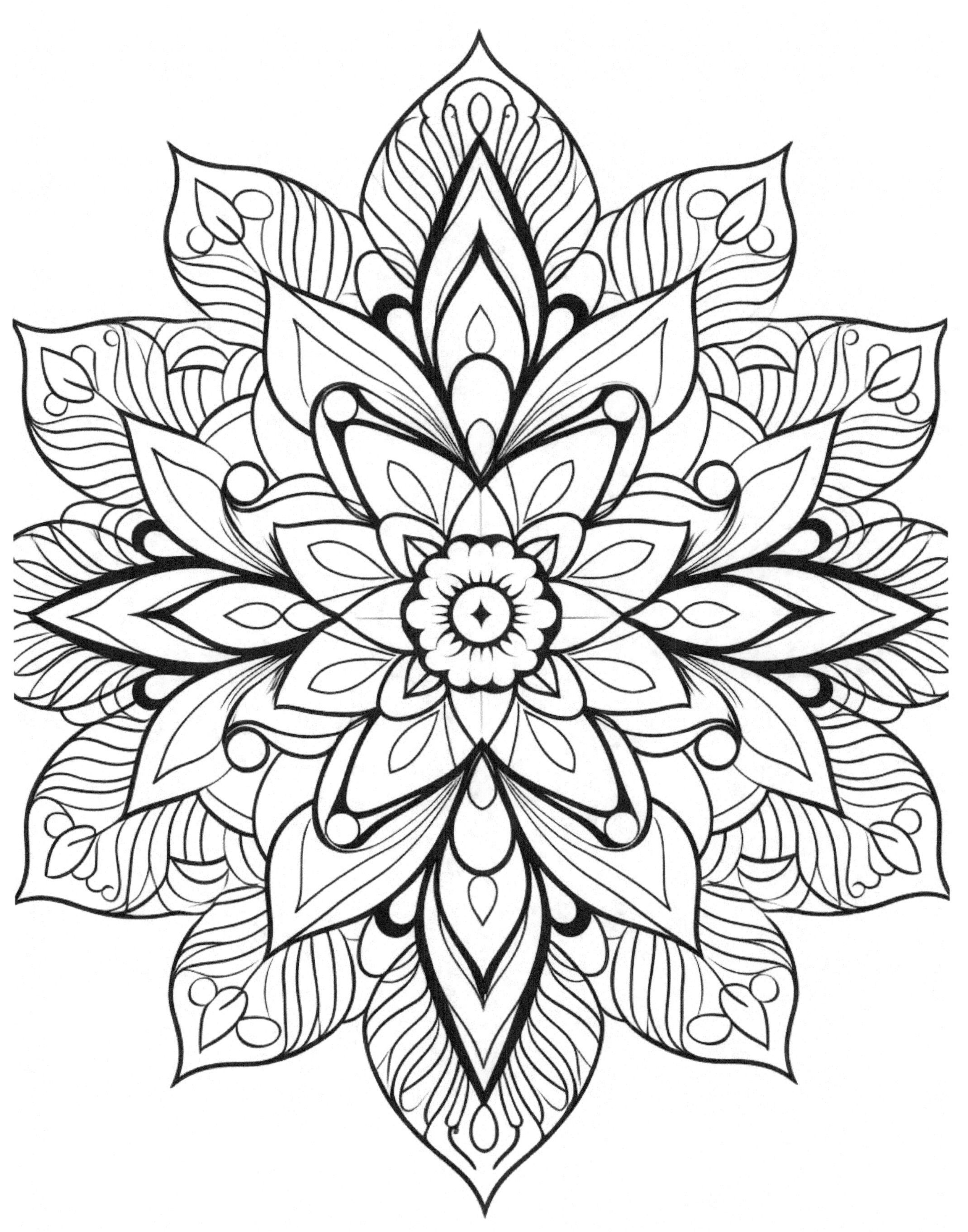

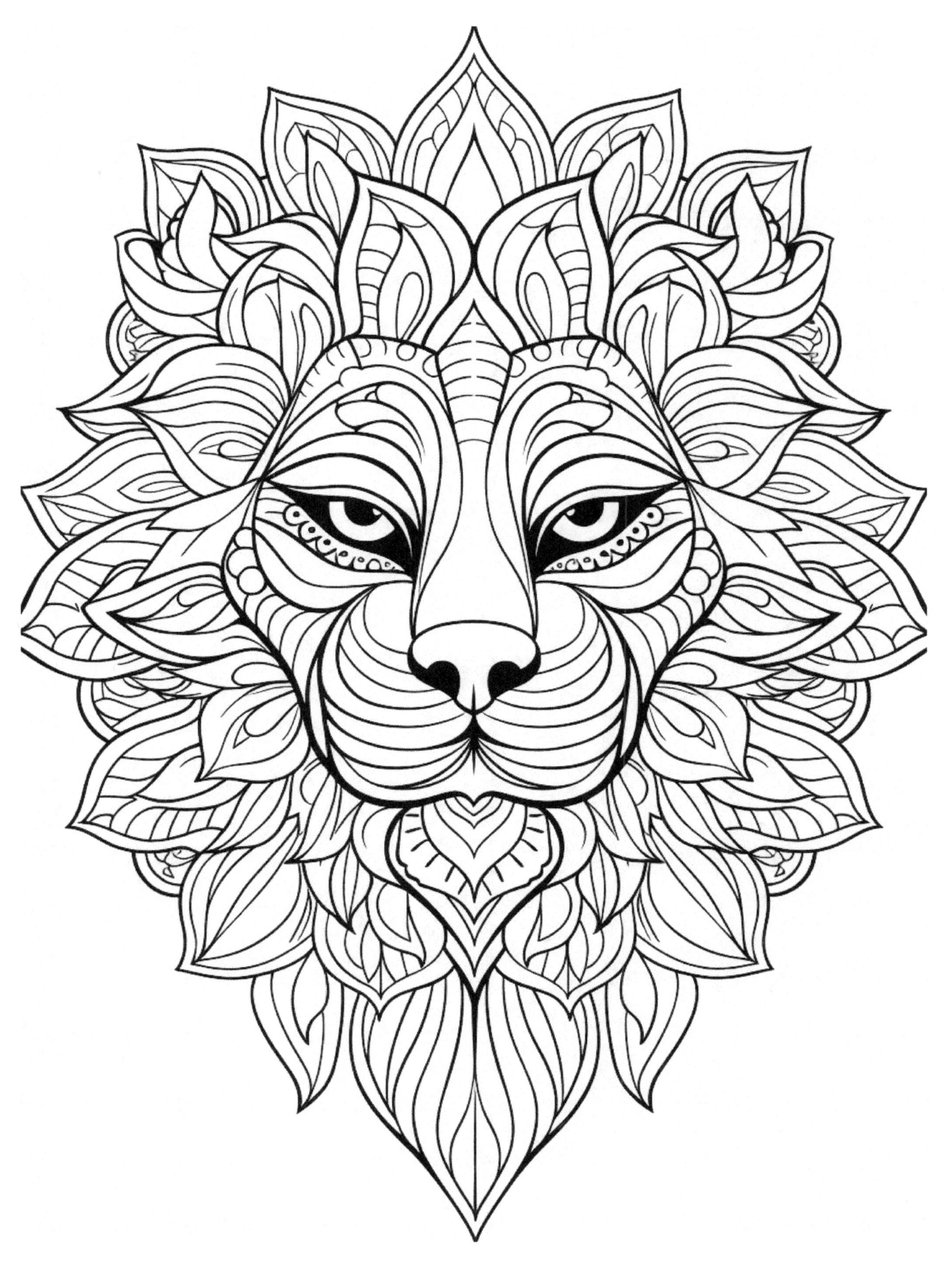

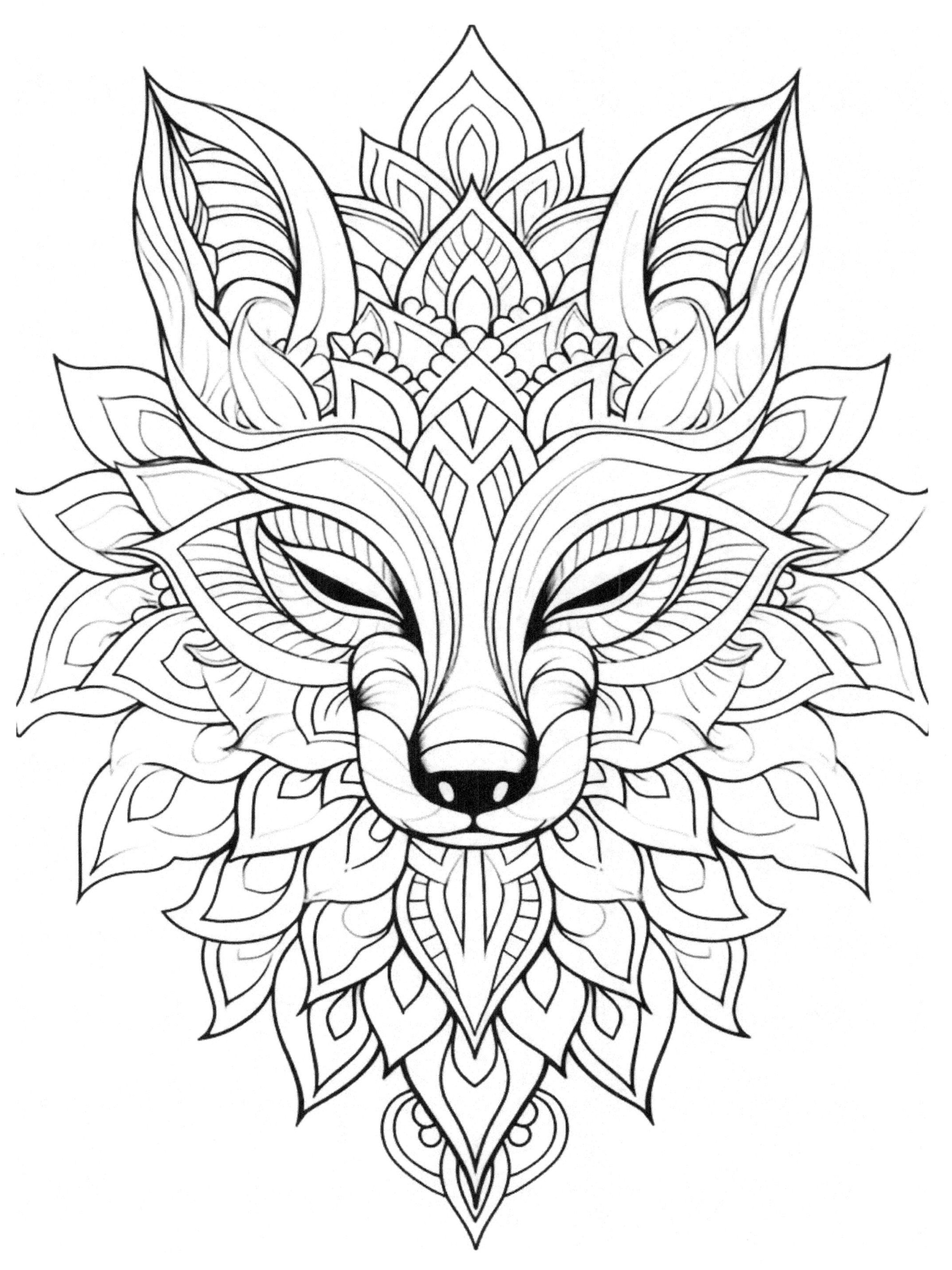

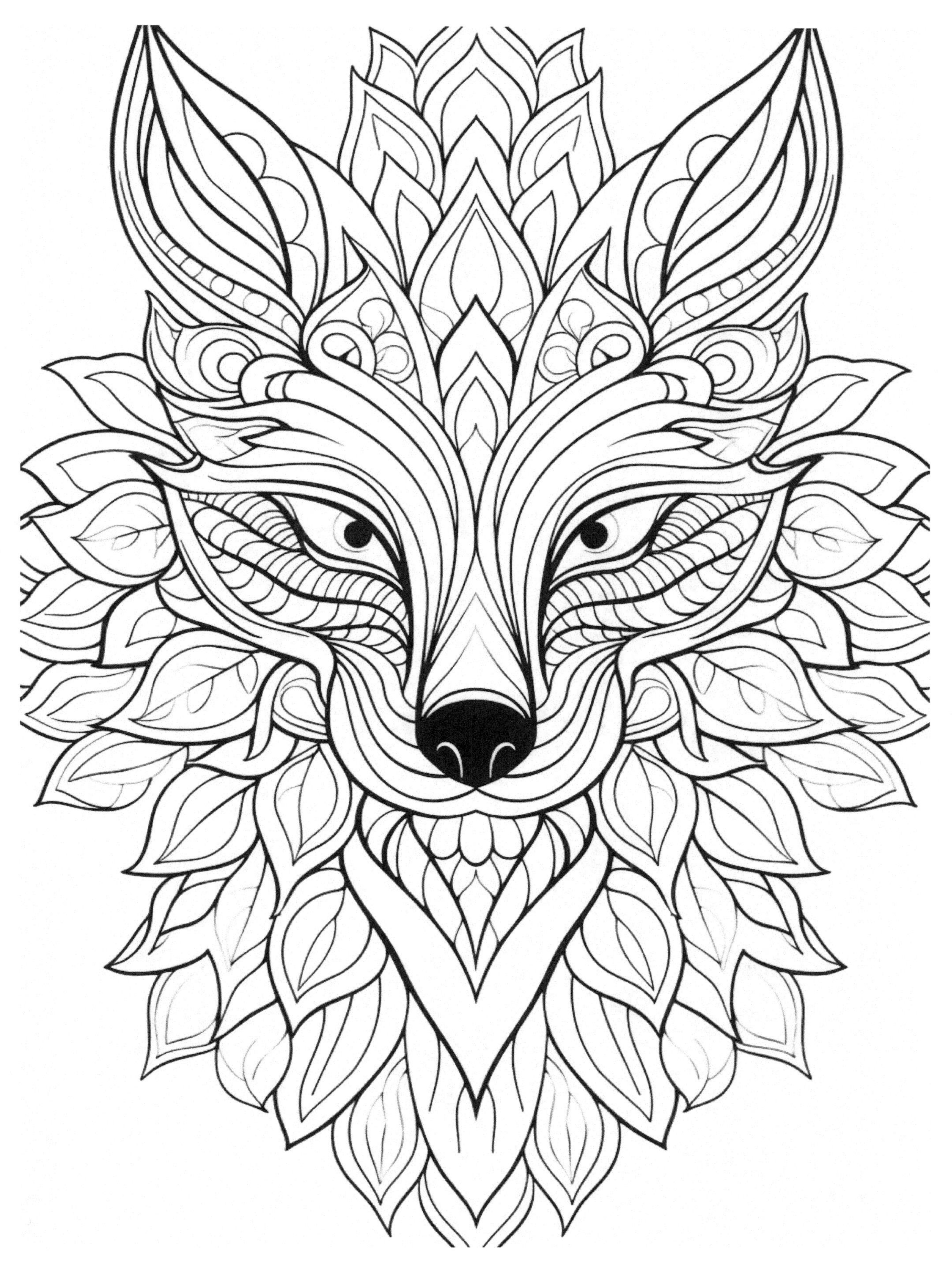

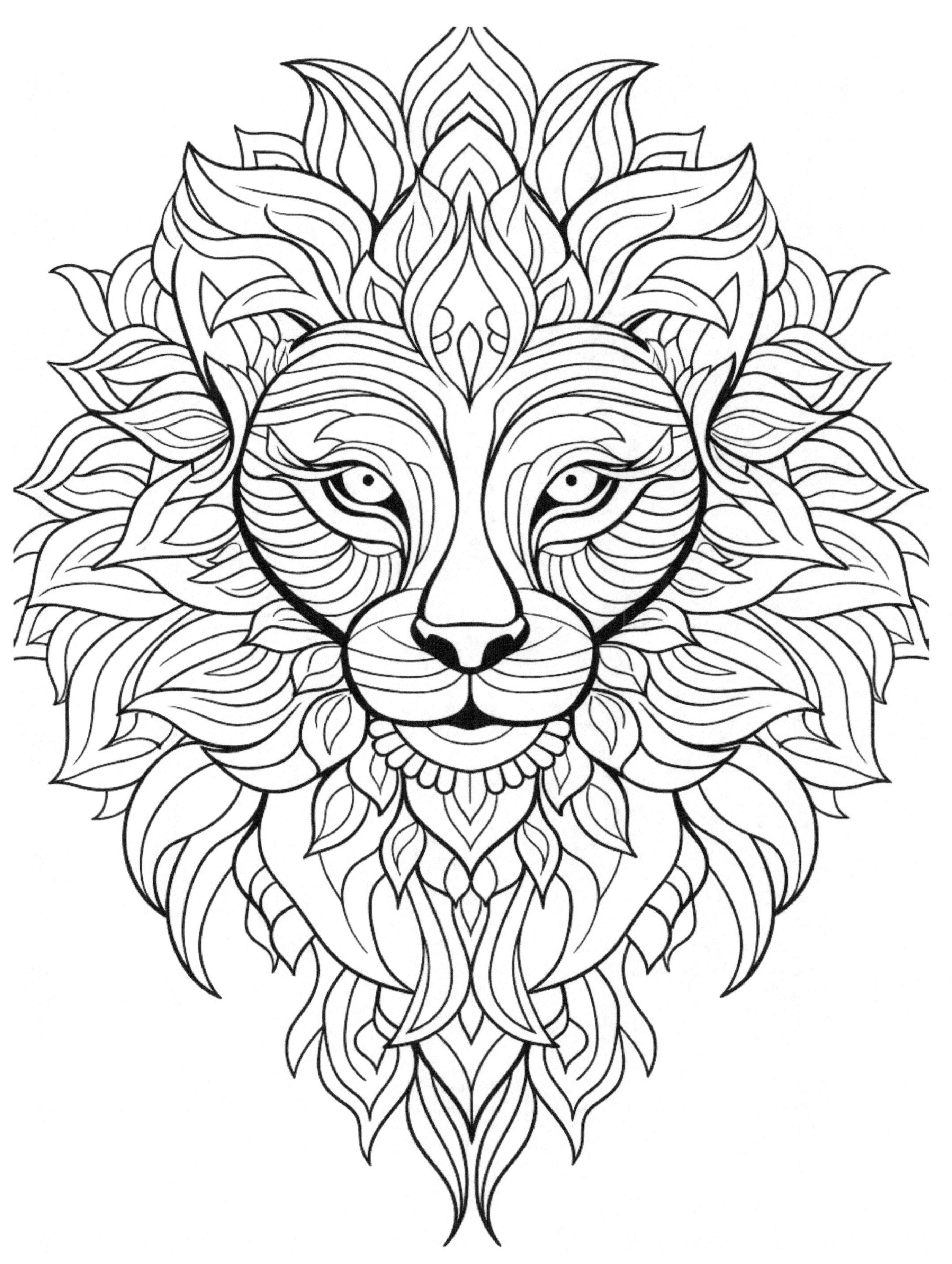

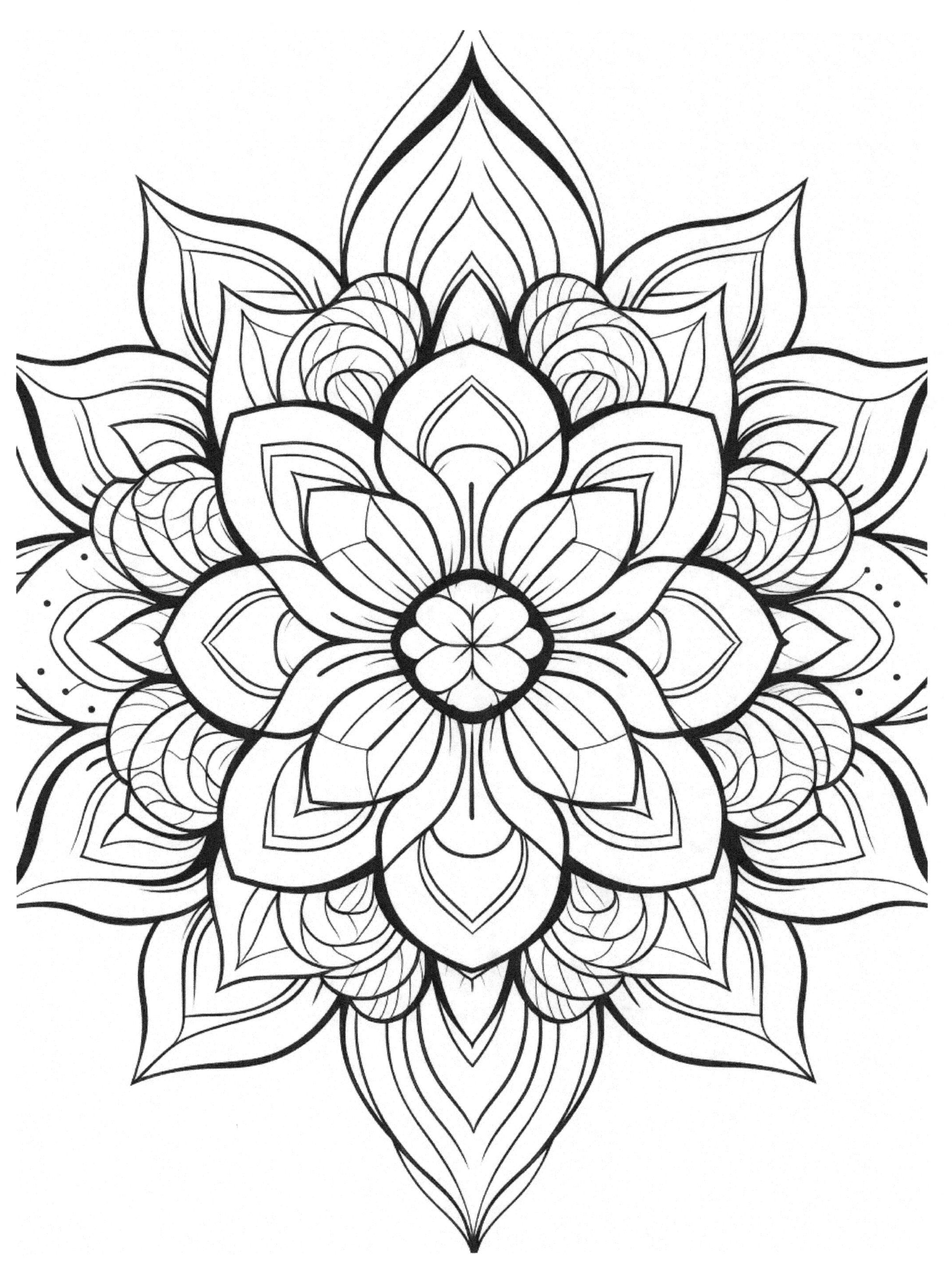

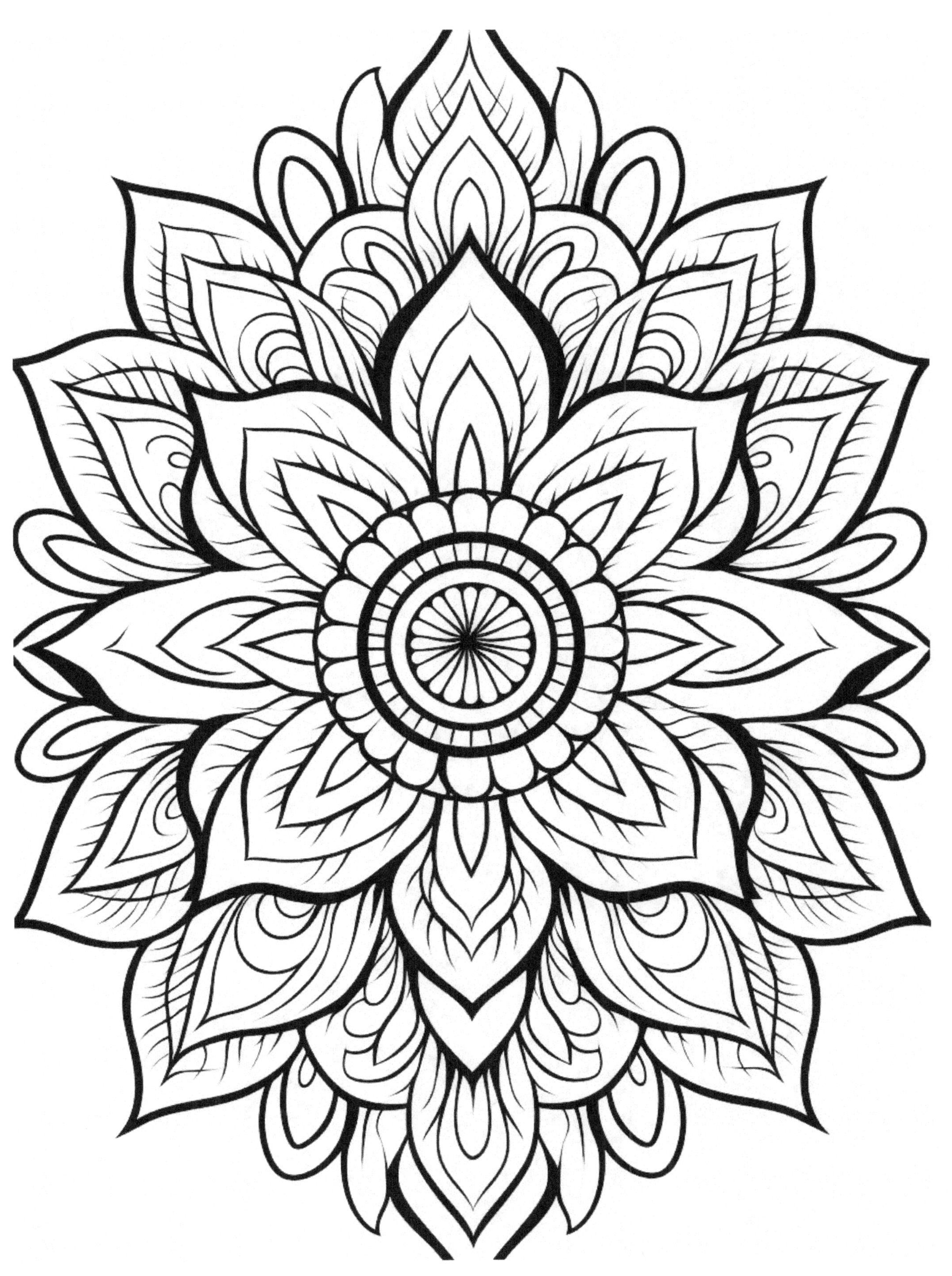

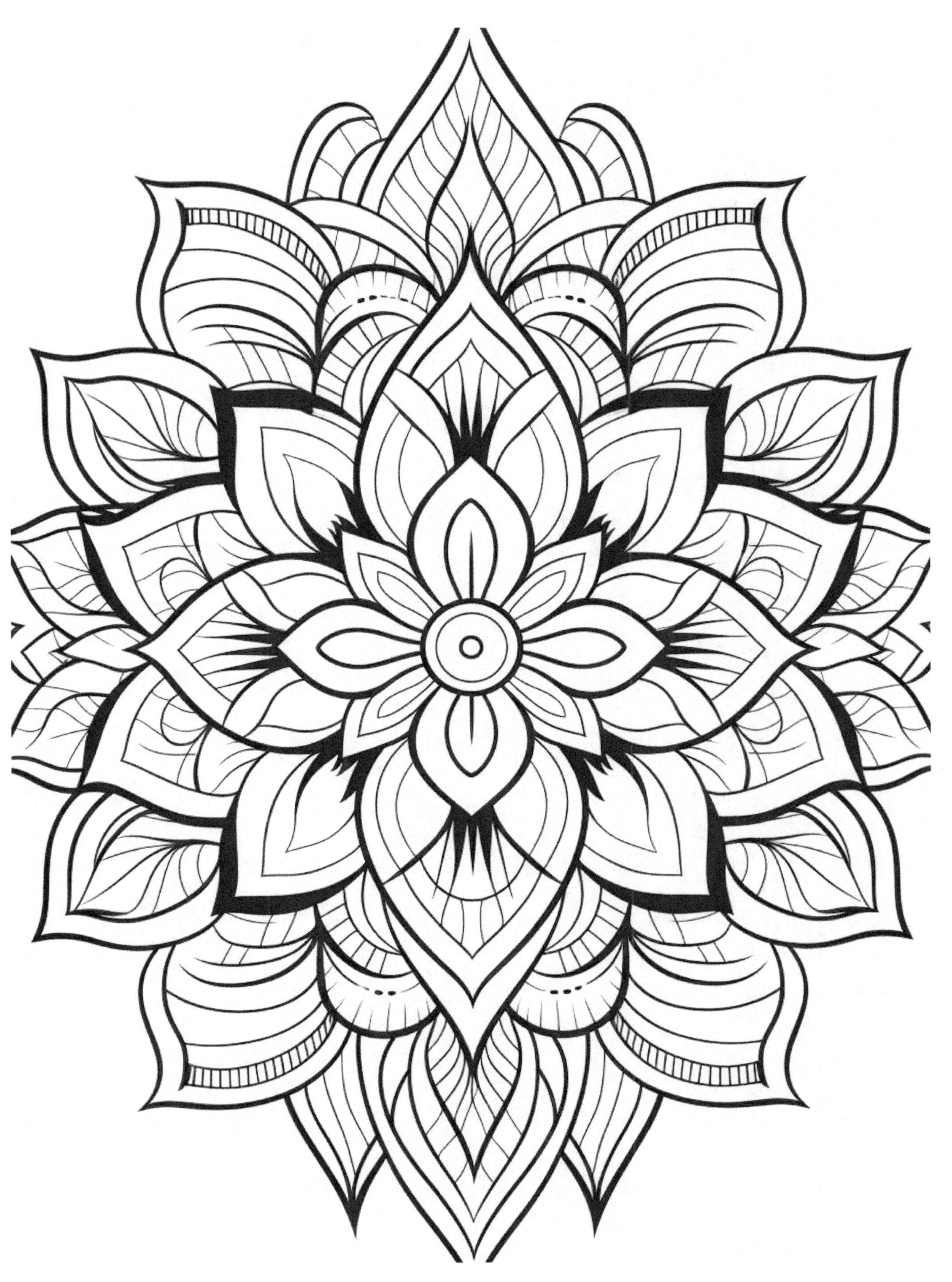

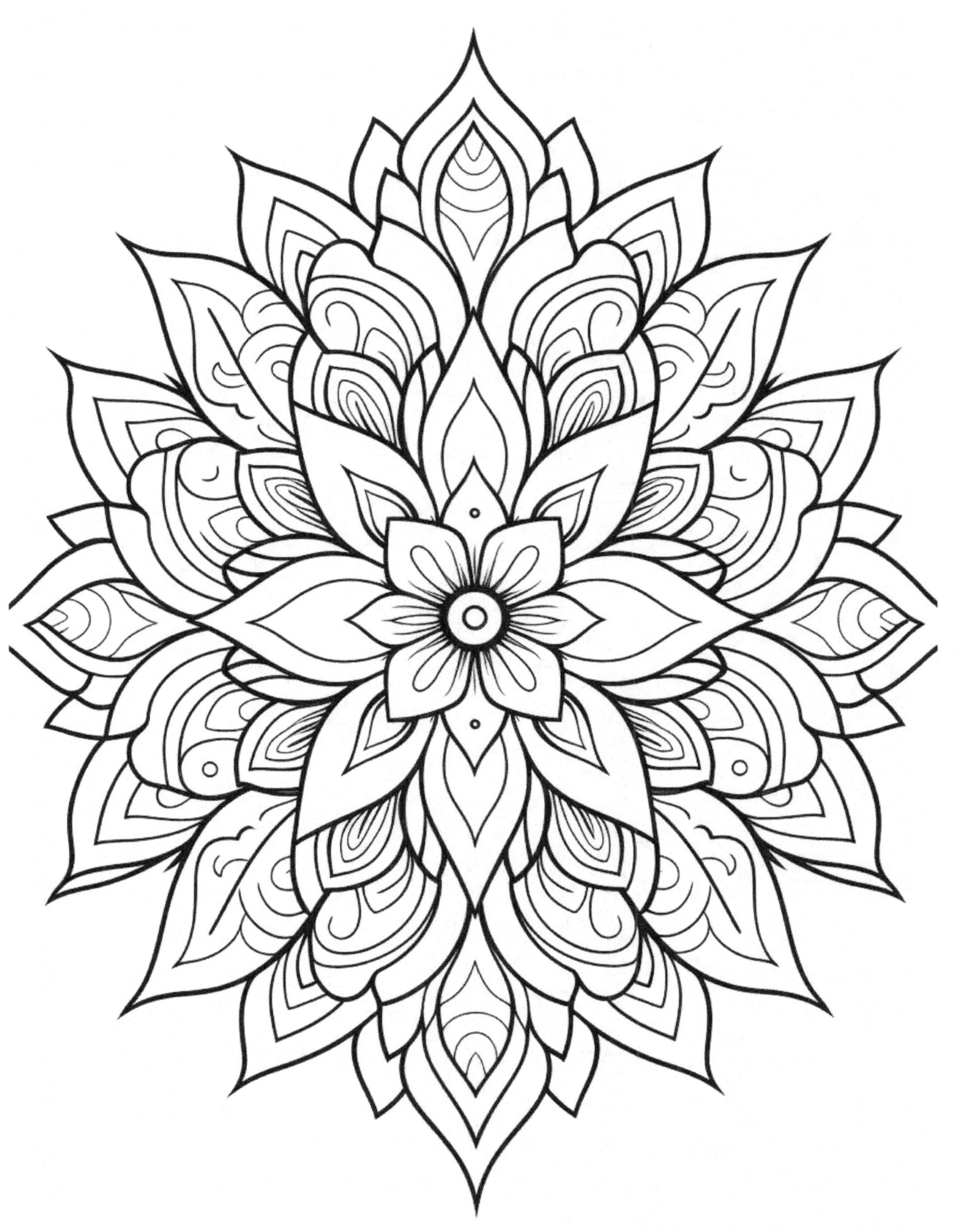

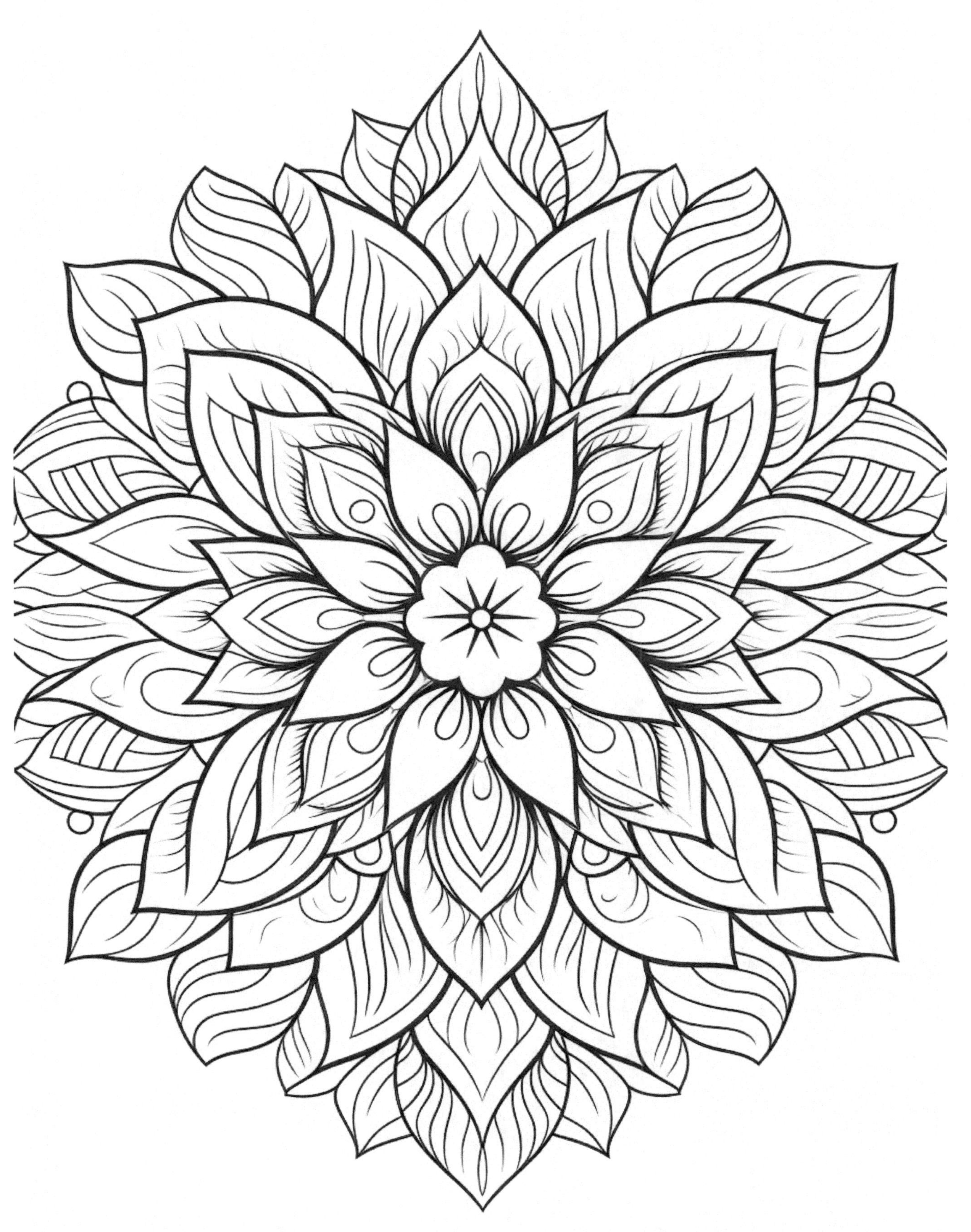

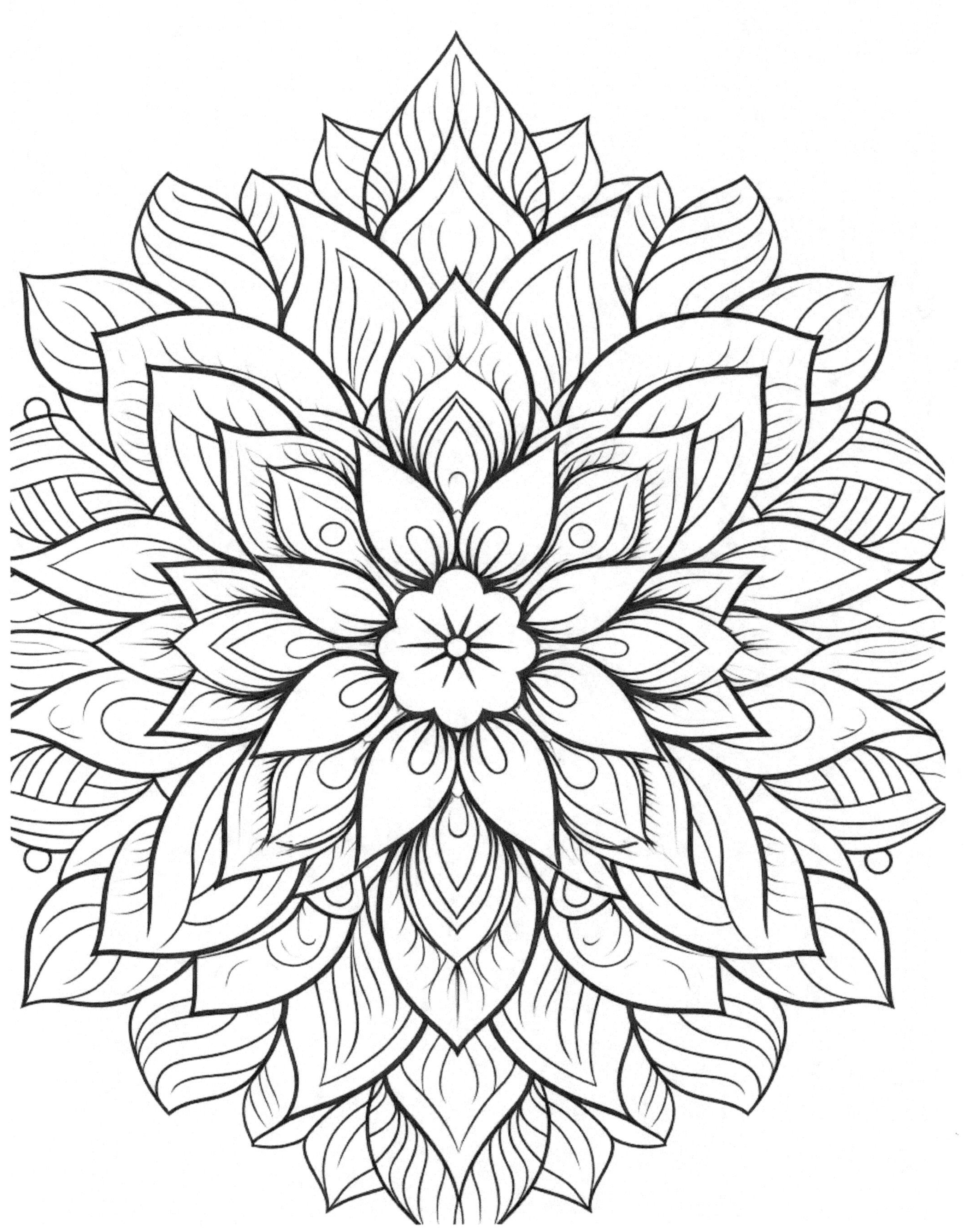

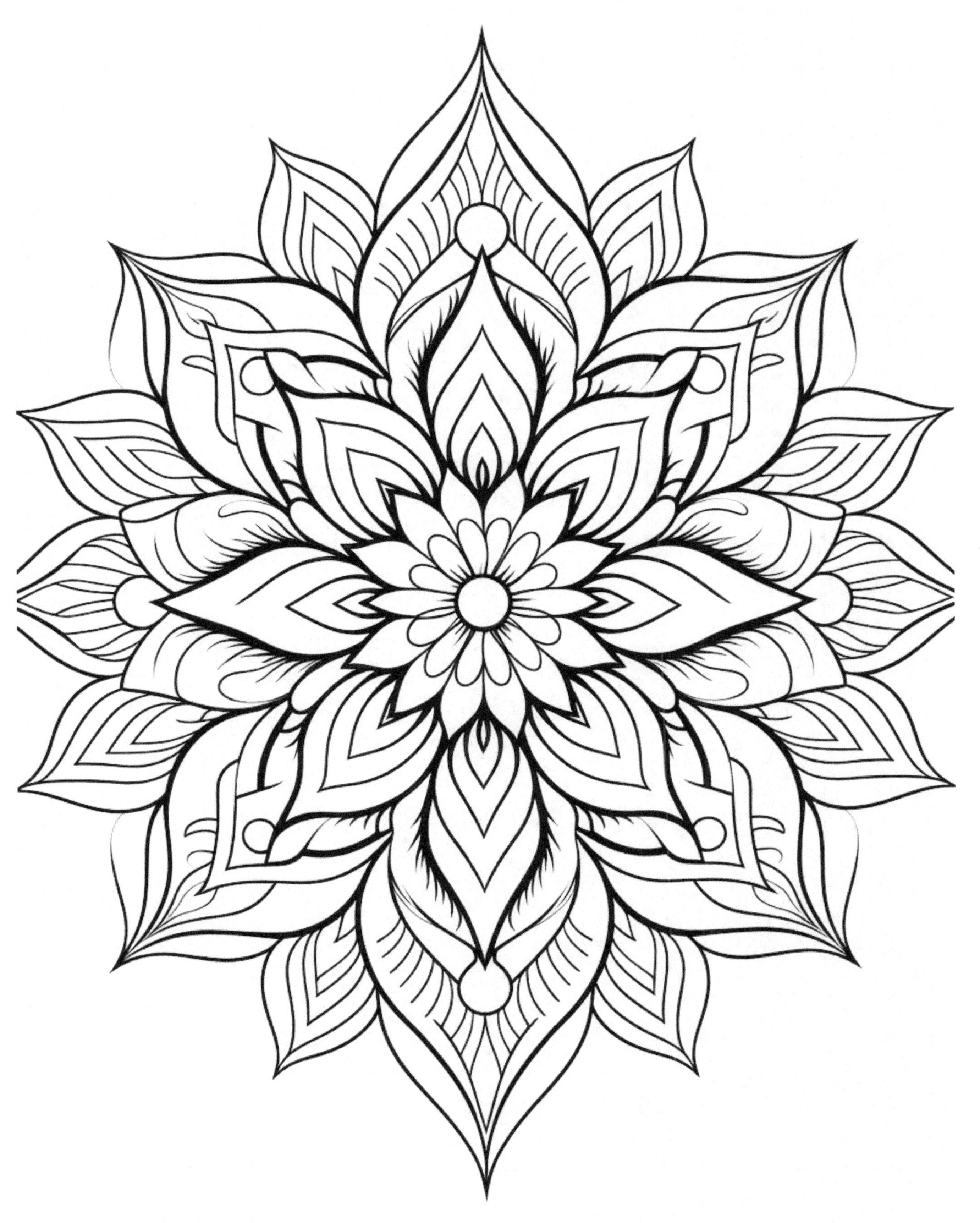

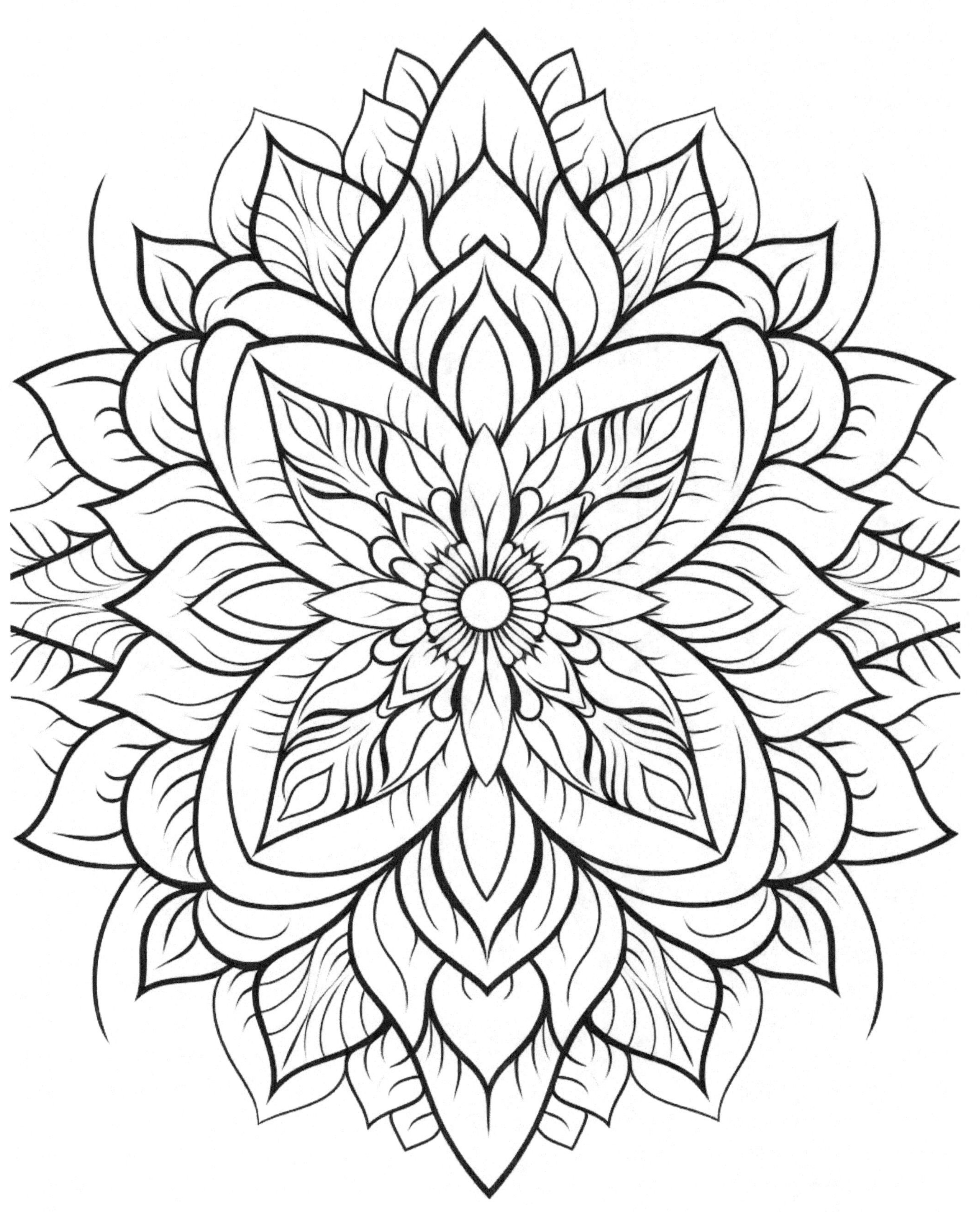

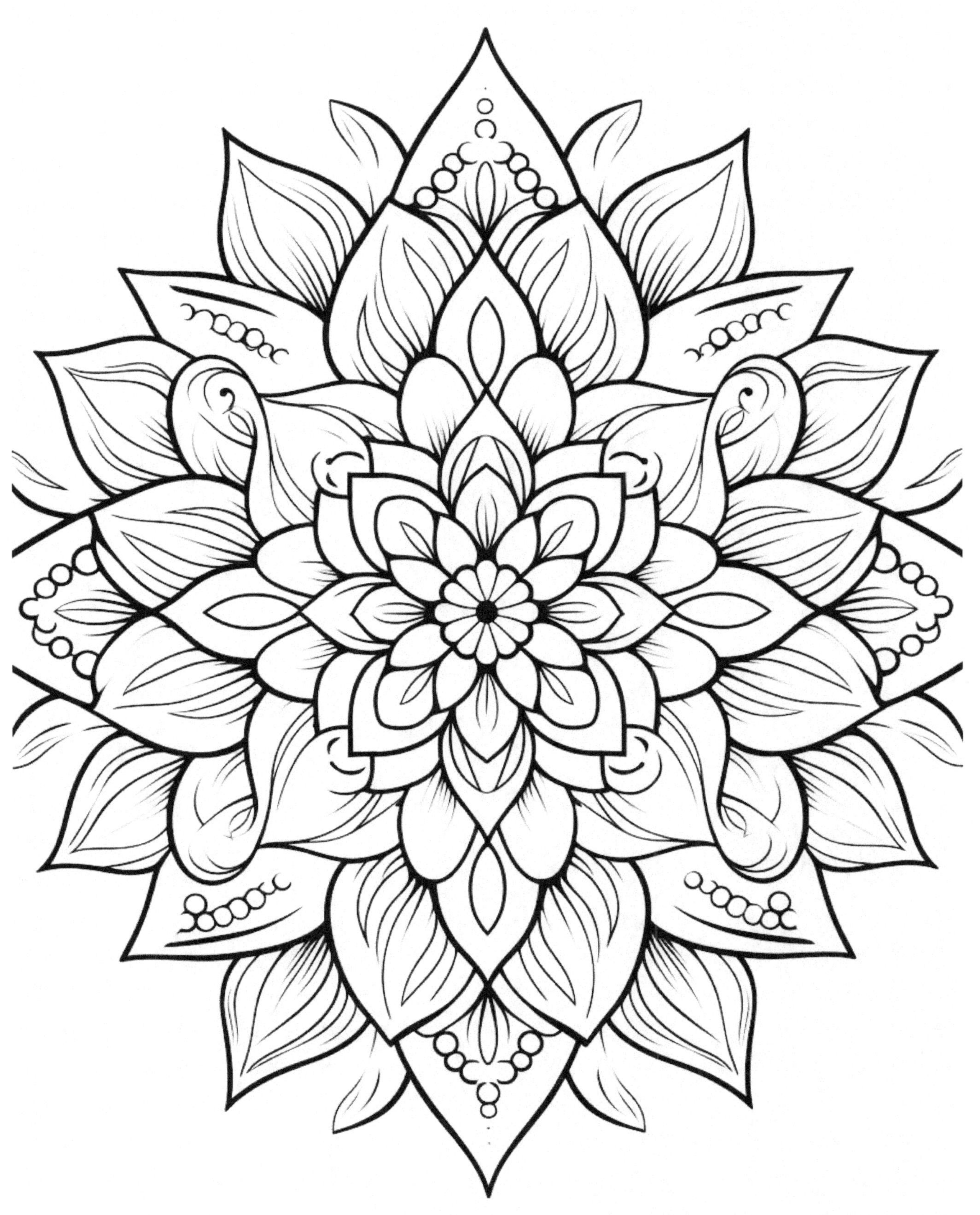

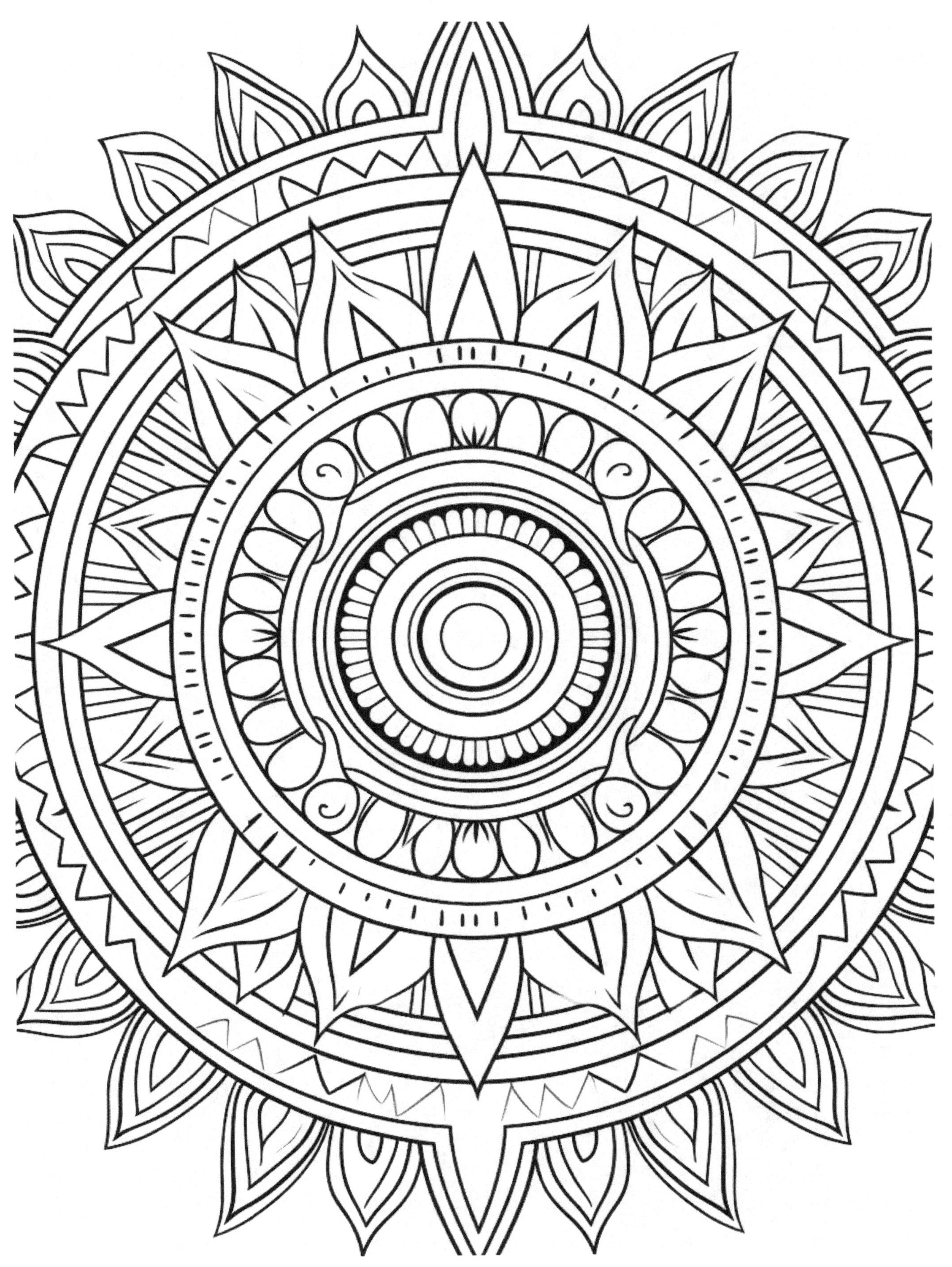

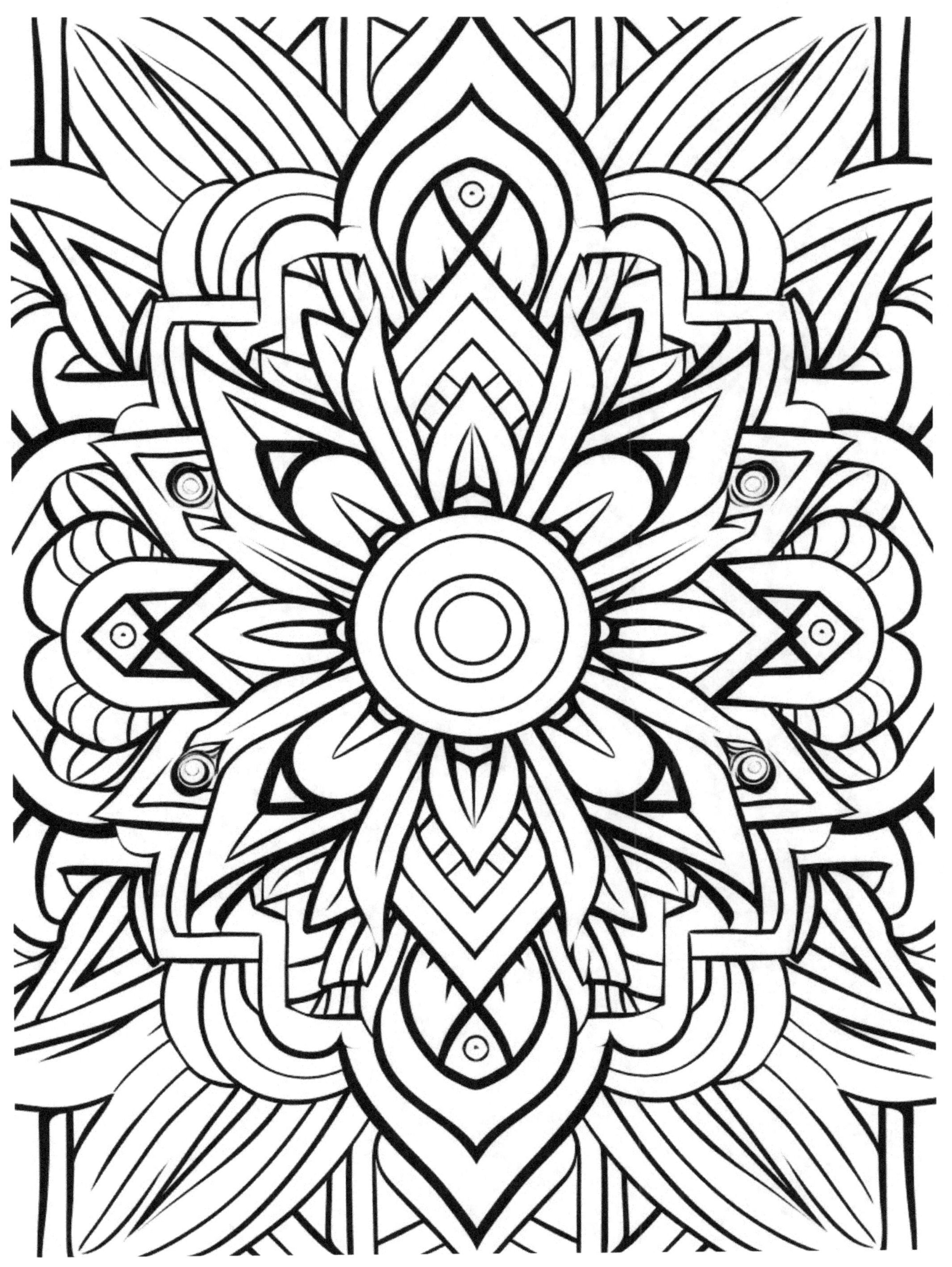

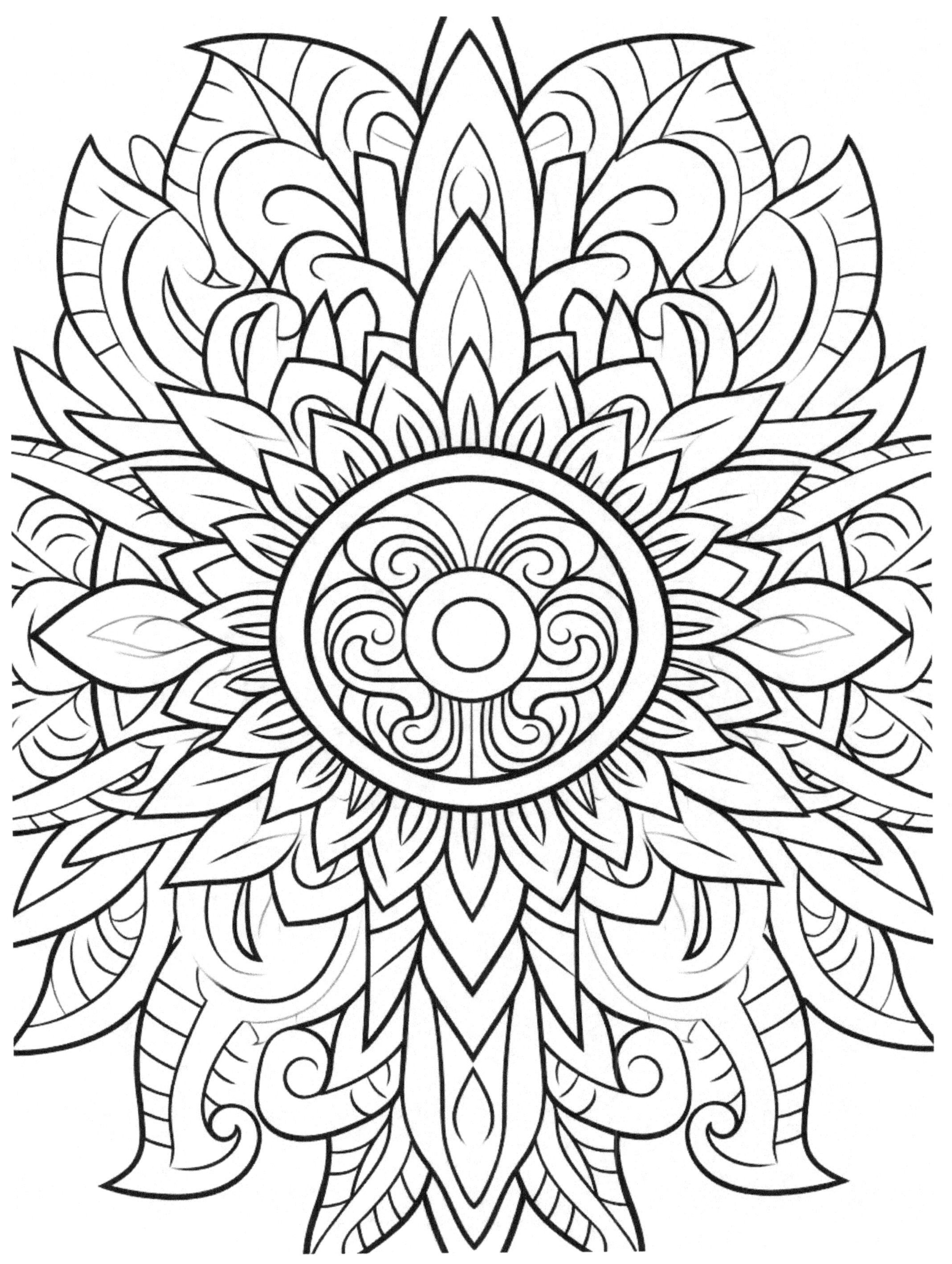

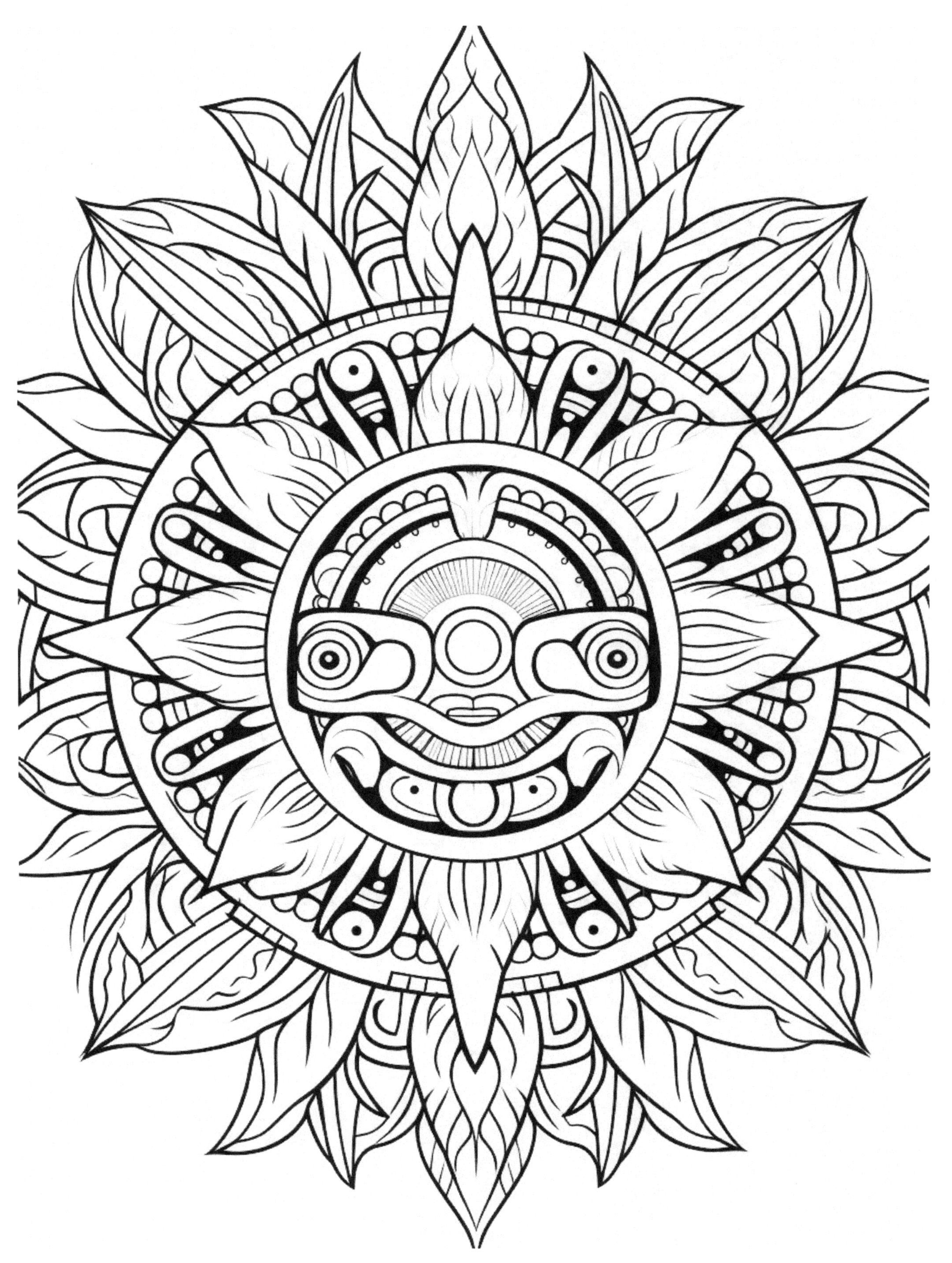